THEMATIC UNIT

Astronomy

Written by Ruth M. Young, M.S. Ed.

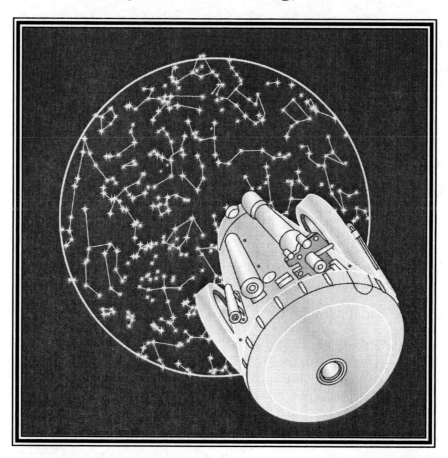

Teacher Created Resources, Inc.
6421 Industry Way
Westminster CA 92683
www.teachercreated.com
ISBN 13: 978-1-57690-622-4
©*2000 Teacher Created Resources, Inc.*
Reprinted, 2007
Made in U.S.A.

Edited by
Walter Kelly

Illustrated by
Howard Chaney

Cover Art by
Agi Palinay

Teacher Created Resources

Table of Contents

Introduction

Astronomy contains a broad-range thematic unit. Its 80 exciting pages are filled with a wide variety of lesson ideas and reproducible pages designed for use with intermediate and middle school students. This book incorporates three outstanding references: *The Young Astronomer*, *The Visual Dictionary of the Universe*, and *Guide to Space*. Other related books are suggested in the annotated resources section.

The activities within each chapter are like threads on a loom, weaving together to enable the students to develop their understanding of science concepts related to astronomy. The threads used in this weaving include all areas of the curriculum. Many of these activities are done in cooperative learning groups to encourage students to exchange and develop their ideas and projects as a team. Where appropriate, various activities are based on material found on the Internet.

This thematic unit contains the following:

❑ **literature selections**—summaries of three books related to the topic of astronomy

❑ **planning guidance**—lessons and activities sequenced to provide a natural flow of study which increases understanding of various concepts related to astronomy

❑ **bulletin boards**—suggestions and instructions for related and interactive bulletin boards

❑ **home/school connections**—ideas for extending the learning into the students' homes

❑ **curriculum connections**—activities which appropriately interweave science with math, language arts, and social studies

❑ **group projects**—activities which foster cooperative learning and expansion of ideas

❑ **technology**—activities which use related Web sites to extend learning and introduce students to current scientific information

❑ **culminating activity**—experiences which require students to apply their learning to create an interesting and informative product that can be shared with others and also serve as alternative assessment for student progress and understanding

❑ **resource section**—an extensive annotated list of information about books and sources of materials specifically related to this study of astronomy

❑ **answer key**—answers for activities used in this unit

Using Internet Connections

Our students are rapidly approaching the real world where knowledge of technological advances is a must. This is particularly important with respect to using the Internet. It is extremely important to be sure that students are using Web sites written by qualified individuals or organizations that can provide them with accurate, current information. Web sites are used throughout this book to extend student learning. These sites have been checked for accuracy, appropriate level of information, and correlation with the subject matter.

Web sites may not always be available; therefore, it is a good idea to use software which enables you to download a single Web page or even an entire Web site, including the links and graphics. Once the Web sites have been downloaded, they can be used again.

Book Summaries

The Visual Dictionary of the Universe
by Sue Becklake

Dorling Kindersley Publishing, Inc. (1993)

The extraordinary visuals throughout this book add information which enhances the topics covered in *The Young Astronomer.* They include spectacular images taken by conventional telescopes and also by the Hubble Space Telescope. Charts and diagrams are provided of star fields and research data. These are all done in such a manner that students will be able to understand them.

The topics covered include the universe, galaxies, stars, planets, asteroids, comets, and meteoroids. Detailed cutaway views of each planet will develop students' knowledge of their physical characteristics. Comparisons of the planets are made possible, using this clearly illustrated information. This book also includes extensive astronomical data and a glossary of astronomical terms.

The Young Astronomer
by Harry Ford

Dorling Kindersley Publishing, Inc. (1998)

This great book is designed for the beginning astronomer, especially those of middle school age. The author is a planetarium lecturer at the old observatory in Greenwich, England. He began looking at the sky at about age 10 when he first saw the rings around Saturn through a small telescope. The topics and activities he includes in this book develop a strong foundation for understanding astronomical history, objects, and events.

A brief history of astronomy is provided, starting with the ancient Greeks in about 180 B.C. to modern astronomy and discoveries made using the Hubble Space Telescope. Equipment is described which can come in handy during astronomical observations. Activities are included which invite the reader to construct a telescope, make a scale model of the planets, and observe the moon.

Guide to Space: A Photographic Journey Through the Universe
by Peter Bond

Dorling Kindersley Publishing, Inc. (1999)

Guide to Space is an outstanding book with current pictures from the Hubble Telescope, satellite pictures, and illustrations depicting a wide range of astronomical topics. When combined with The Visual Dictionary of the Universe, extensive information is provided for middle grade and higher students. The easy-to-read text brings the latest information about the planets, moon, man's exploration of the moon, comets and asteroids, and stars.

A list of space Web sites can be found in the Space Data section at the end of the book. These include a variety of sites such as **Deep-Space Missions, European Space Agency, Japanese Space Program, and Sky and Telescope magazine.**

Scale Models

Scale Model of the Solar System (*The Visual Dictionary of the Universe*, pages 26 and 27)

The dimensions of the solar system are best demonstrated by using string to represent the distance of the planets from the sun. The drawing in *The Visual Dictionary of the Universe* shows the orbits divided into inner and outer planets. A scale model of the solar system shows this division, as well as the enormous distances between planets.

Activity: creating a scale model of the solar system

Materials: 300 ft. (100 m) of heavy string; nine pieces of heavy cardboard, 5 in. x 8 in. (12.5 cm x 20 cm); nine metal washers; nine meter sticks; scissors

- Divide the students into nine groups and assign each group a planet. Using the following chart, have students cut strings to represent the distance of each planet from the sun.

Planet	Actual Distance from Sun		Length of String
	in millions of miles	in kilometers	in meters
Mercury	36	58	.4
Venus	67	108	.7
Earth	93	150	1.0
Mars	142	228	1.5
Jupiter	484	779	5.2
Saturn	897	1,434	9.6
Uranus	1,785	2,873	19.2
Neptune	2,793	4,495	30.0
Pluto	3,647	870	39.3
Scale: Earth's distance from the sun = 1 meter (Astronomers call this distance an *Astronomical Unit*—AU.)			

- Next, on a piece of cardboard each group should print the name of its planet and distance from the sun. A hole should be punched at one edge of this card and the length of string tied to it. Tie the washer to the string end to prevent it from fraying.

- Select one student to represent the sun by standing against the wall in front of the class. Have a member of each of the first four groups hand the washer to the "sun" and then stretch out the strings across the front of the classroom. Do this one at a time (in the order on the chart) so students can see how close these four planets are.

- Have the Jupiter group add their string to this line-up. Students will see the gap between it and Mars—the space between the inner and outer planets. Scientists think asteroids within this space remain from the early formation of our solar system.

- It will now be obvious that the outer planet strings cannot be stretched out inside the classroom. Move outside, have the first four planet strings stretched out again, and let five more students stretch out the strings for the rest of the outer planets.

Scale Models *(cont.)*

- Have the strings placed on the ground so students can all walk the scale model solar system. Explain that on this scale, the nearest star (beyond the sun) would be about 174 miles (2,784 km) away! Also ask them what the sun would look like from the most distant planet, Pluto. (It would just be a bright star, so distant that its heat does not reach Pluto.)

- Return to the classroom and show the solar system pictures on pages 26-27 in *The Visual Dictionary of the Universe*. Point out the following information:

    1. The orbits of the inner planets are clustered closer to the sun than the outer ones.

    2. Excepting Pluto's, all planets' orbits lie in nearly the same plane as Earth's.

    3. Pluto is inclined 17.2° to Earth's orbital plane. It also passes inside Neptune's orbit, but there is no danger of a collision since they are so far apart. However, it means that Pluto is sometimes closer to the sun than Neptune. This happened recently when Pluto passed inside Neptune's orbit in 1979 and then outside again in 1999.

    4. All planets travel in the same direction around the sun—counterclockwise when viewed from above.

    5. All planets spin in the same counterclockwise direction as their orbits, except Venus, Uranus, and Pluto, which spin in the opposite direction.

    6. The planets do not travel in a straight line extending from the sun. They are spread out like runners around a track. The closer to the sun, the faster the planet travels around it.

Activity: making a graph of the distances of the planets from the sun

Materials: transparency and copies of Plotting Planetary Orbital Distances (page 7)

- Review the activity of using strings to make a scale model of the solar system and the drawing of the solar system in *The Visual Dictionary of the Universe*.

- Explain to the students that they are going to graph the distances of the nine planets from the sun.

- Distribute the graph and discuss the use of astronomical units as distances to be plotted on this graph. Be sure the students are aware that the Astronomical Unit (AU) is based on Earth's distance from the sun. Thus, Earth's AU is one, and the AU's of other planets are more or less than one, depending upon their distances from the sun.

- Have the students follow the instructions to complete the graph.

- Use a transparency of this graph and ask student volunteers to plot the data on it. As this is done, have students check their work. Discuss their findings:

    1. The planets' distances are not equally spaced but increase with the distance of the planets from the sun.

    2. The inner planets are closely grouped near the sun. The outer planets are spread out much farther.

    3. The inner planets are all small and rocky. All the outer planets, except Pluto, are huge gas giants.

Ask students to propose a theory for outer planets' orbits being so much farther apart than those of inner planets. (The sun's gravity holds planets in orbit. As they get farther from the sun, the gravitational pull decreases and their orbits can spread farther apart.)

Scale Models *(cont.)*

Plotting Planetary Orbital Distances

Instructions: Plot the distance from the sun for each planet, using astronomical units as shown in the following chart.

Planet	Astronomical Units
Mercury	.4
Venus	.7
Earth	1.0
Mars	1.5

Planet	Astronomical Units
Jupiter	5.2
Saturn	9.6
Uranus	19.3
Neptune	30.3
Pluto	39.7

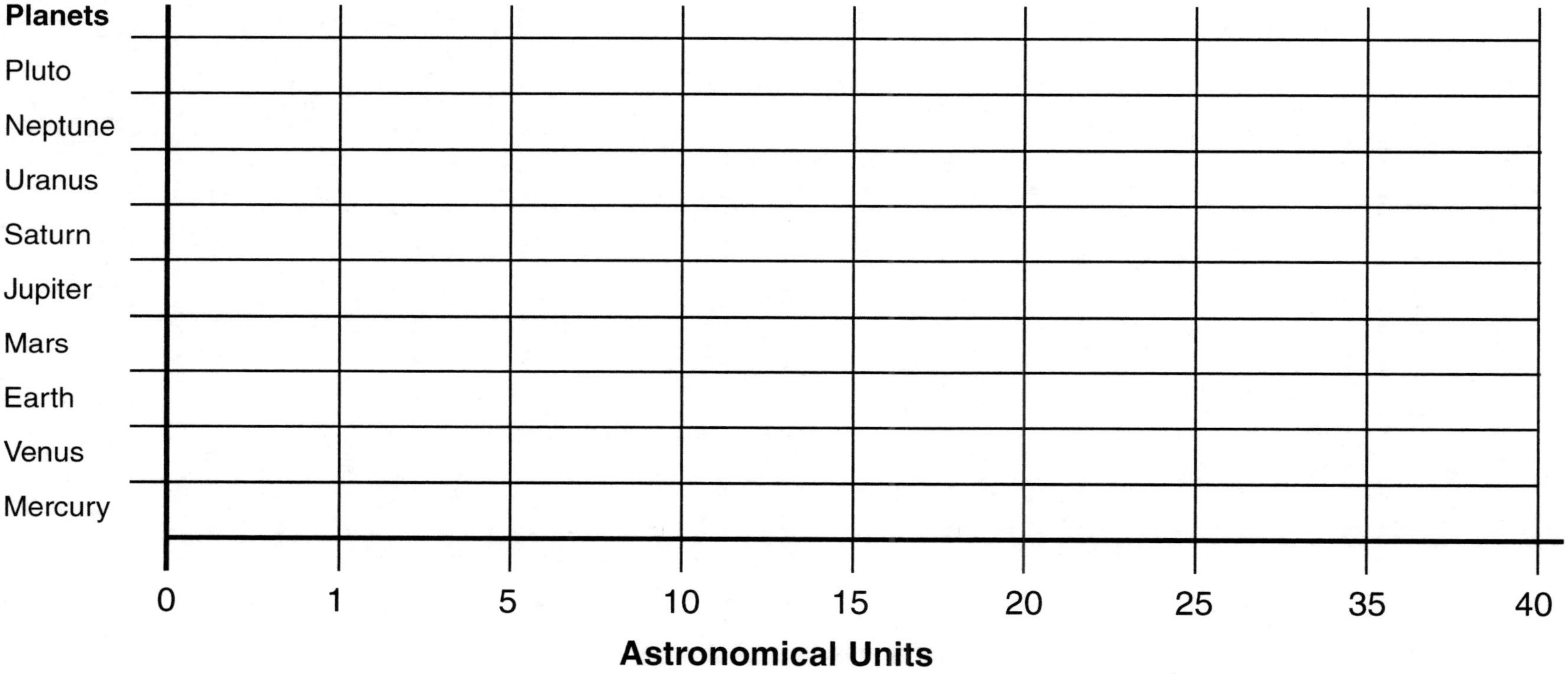

Planets

Pluto
Neptune
Uranus
Saturn
Jupiter
Mars
Earth
Venus
Mercury

0 1 5 10 15 20 25 35 40

Astronomical Units

Scale Models (*cont.*)

Scale Model of the Solar System (*The Young Astronomer;* pages 14 and 15)

The nine planets vary in size from the smallest, Pluto, to the giant gas ball, Jupiter. There are various methods for creating scale models of the planets to help visualize and compare these sizes. One method is by constructing three-dimensional models, as described on pages 14 and 15 of *The Young Astronomer*. If this method is used, the size of Pluto (as shown in the box on page 15) needs to be decreased by slightly more than half since Pluto is much smaller than Mercury. This would require the ball representing Pluto to be .4 in. (10 mm). Painting the tiny planets is impractical, but the larger ones can be painted. A different scale model of the planets is described in the following activity.

Activity: making paper models of the planets

Materials: five small pieces of colored construction paper, four large pieces of 36 in. (90 cm) wide butcher paper, pencil, compass, meter stick, metric ruler, 15 meters of string, four file cards

- Divide the students into nine groups and let each create a scale model of a planet.
- On colored paper, construct models of the smaller planets by using a compass to draw circles with radii as indicated on the chart below. The scale is based upon Earth's diameter of 7,973 miles (12,756 km) being equal to 10 cm.

Smaller Planets

Planet	Actual Diameter		Model Radius	Color
	miles	kilometers	centimeters	
Mercury	3,032	4,879	1.9	gray
Venus	7,521	12,104	4.8	white
Earth	7,926	12,756	5	blue
Mars	4,222	6,794	2.7	red
Pluto	1,485	2,390	0.9	black
Scale: Earth's diameter = 10 cm				

- Since their radii will be too large to be drawn with a compass, the larger planets will be drawn on butcher paper. To fit the butcher paper, Jupiter and Saturn will be half circles only. Use compasses made from string to draw these large circles. Measure the strings to the length of each planet's radius, as shown on the chart on page nine, allowing a bit of extra string to tie a loop at one end. Punch a hole in the edge of each file card and tie the planet string through it. Tie a loop in the other end of the string.

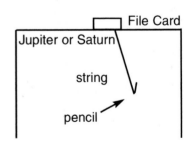

- Lay the card on the butcher paper—in the center to make full circles for Neptune and Uranus, and at the edge to make the half circles for Jupiter and Saturn. Place a large pin through the hole in the card and into the butcher paper and a piece of cardboard under it. One student holds the pin while another stretches out the string, using a pencil in the looped end. A circle or half circle is then drawn for the planet.

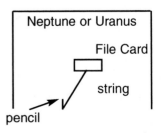

8   © *Teacher Created Resources, Inc.*

Scale Models *(cont.)*

Giant Planets

Planet	Actual Diameter		Model Radius	Color
	miles	kilometers	centimeters	
Jupiter	88,846	142,984	56 cm	red or orange
Saturn	74,897	120,536	47 cm	yellow
Uranus	31,763	51,118	20 cm	green
Neptune	30,775	4,928	19.5 cm	blue
Scale: Earth's diameter = 10 cm				

Comparing the Models

- Have students cut out their planet models and compare sizes. Fold the Earth model in half and let students guess how many times it will fit across the diameter of Jupiter. Let them check the guess by starting the model at the edge of Jupiter and counting how many times it can be moved across the diameter (about 11 times). Let the students also compare the sizes of the other planets to one another (e.g., Mars to Earth).

- Let students use pictures of planets on pages 30-47 in *The Visual Dictionary of the Universe* to help them draw the features on their models. Other sources for planet pictures are Web sites and *Our Universe* (see Resources section of this book).

- Paper rings should be added to the giant planets—Jupiter, Saturn, Uranus, and Neptune. Use pictures to show the rings. Have students note that rings vary in width as well as tilt, relative to each planet's own tilt on its axis. The rings generally circle the equator of each planet.

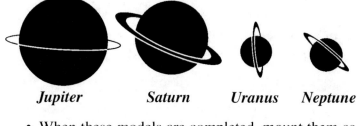

Jupiter   *Saturn*   *Uranus*   *Neptune*

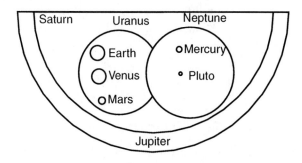

- When these models are completed, mount them as shown in the drawing.

- Cut a string to equal the length of the sun's diameter, using the same scale as that of the planets. The sun is 868,750 miles (1,390,000 km) in diameter; thus, the string should be 9.3 meters long. Have two students hold the planet models while another stretches the sun string along the diameter of Jupiter out to its full length. This should be done outside since the string will extend beyond the classroom.

- Mount the planets on a bulletin board to remain during this unit. Stretch the sun's string along the diameter of Jupiter and then out to full length, even though this requires winding it around the classroom wall.

Planetary Features

Physical Features: (*The Visual Dictionary of the Universe*, pages 30-35 and 38-47; *Guide to Space*, pages 12-37)

These two books depict a great deal of information regarding each of the nine planets. Drawings illustrate surface features as well as interior views and atmosphere structure and composition. The data for planetary diameters in these books are not current. Use the Planetary Facts found in the Appendix of this book (page 75) for the latest data.

Activity: describing the physical features of the planets

Materials: large Styrofoam balls, paint, felt pens, meat skewers, calculators, Planetary Features Summary (page 11)

- Divide students into nine groups, assigning each group a planet to research and to present to the rest of the class. Discuss ways their presentations can help the class learn about the planets.

These may include the following:

1. using color transparencies of images from *The Visual Dictionary of the Universe*
2. using color printouts of pictures from Web sites
3. using Solar System Lithograph, set EP338 8/95 from NASA or JPL (see Resources section, page 77. The set includes 8" x 10" pictures and information about the planets, sun, moon, and asteroids.)
4. using a model of the planet made from half a Styrofoam ball to show the interior layers

    A. painting the sections of the layers, writing descriptions of the layers on small paper flags
    B. using straight pins to place the flags on the model
    C. pushing a meat skewer through the center of the Styrofoam model to represent its axis and mounting the model on a block of wood to show the angle of inclination of the planet
    D. placing a layer of modeling clay around the outside of the planet model to show some of the surface features and painting the surface to represent colored pictures of the planet

- Distribute copies of the Planetary Features Summary to each group and review it with them.

- Determine a time line enabling groups to gather and prepare their information. Copyright dates on any resource books should be within five years to avoid outdated information.

- Have the students visit the following Web sites:

    Geology of the Terrestrial Planets (Mercury, Venus, Earth and Mars only)
    http://www-glg.la.asu.edu/~glg_intro/planetary/01_start_planet.htm
    Several views of the planets taken by satellites are available. Students should look at all the views of each planet.

    Views of the Solar System
    The following Web sites provide recent and accurate information.
    http://pds.jpl.nasa.gov/planets/
    http://www.solarviews.com/eng/homepage.htm
    Keyword: Planets

Planetary Features Summary

Instructions: Record the data about your planet on this form and use it as you develop your presentation. Use several resources to get this information, always checking the copyright date as well as the author of the material. The copyright date should be within five years, and the authors should be scientists or reliable agencies such as NASA. (National Aeronautics and Space Administration)

Planet Name _____

- order from the sun _____
- average distance from the sun _____
- length of time to revolve around the sun once _____
- type of planet (rocky or gaseous) _____
- tilt of the axis of the planet to the plane of its orbit _____ °
- direction it rotates on its axis (clockwise or counterclockwise) _____
- surface temperatures _____ ° to _____ °
- composition of the atmosphere _____
- unusual surface features _____

Reference Sources (Books and Periodicals)				
Author(s)	**Title**	**Publisher**	**Date**	**Page(s)**

Web Sites	
Title	**URL** http://

Planet Projects

Planetary Motion (*The Young Astronomer*, pages 16 and 17)

Not all planets are perfect spheres. The gas giants (Jupiter, Saturn, Uranus, and Neptune) tend to oblate, or flatten at the top and bottom, making their equators larger than the distances between the poles. This is caused by their rapid rotation and gaseous structure. After determining the rotation speed of the planets (below), use the instruction pages 16 and 17 to construct a scale model of how this rapid spinning changes the shapes of the giant gas planets.

Activity: determining the rotation speed of the planets

Materials: metric tape measure and ruler, pencil compass, tagboard, calculator, How Fast Do Planets Spin? (page 13)

- Ask the students how long it takes Earth to rotate once around its axis (24 hours). Tell the students that all planets do not rotate at this same speed. Explain that they are going to do an activity in which they will learn to calculate the speed of a planet.

- Have students work in small groups and distribute a copy of How Fast Do Planets Spin? to each group. Use the transparency to review the instructions.

- Distribute a tape measure, ruler, compass, calculator, and pieces of tagboard to each group. Monitor them as they draw the four circles and complete the chart as instructed on the work sheet. When all groups have finished the chart, ask them to share their results. Be sure they know that the ratio of the circumference to the diameter = 3.14 (π)

- Have students calculate the rotation speed of Earth, using the formula and then recording it on the chart. Let groups share results to be sure they all agree.

- Have them complete calculations for the rotation speeds of the other eight planets.

- Help the students analyze this data by having them do the following:

  1. List the planets in order, from the fastest to the slowest rotation speeds.

  2. List the planets in order according to their diameters, with the largest first.

  3. Discuss what you find by comparing the size of the planet to its rotation speed. (The largest planets spin more rapidly than the smaller planets.)

- Tell students they will make a model to demonstrate how the rapid spinning of the giant planets changes their shape. Provide each group with the materials listed in the activity in *The Young Astronomer* and show them how to assemble these.

Spin the model of Jupiter between your hands to see it flatten out (*oblate*).

Planet Projects *(cont.)*

How Fast Do Planets Spin?

Earth is shaped like a sphere. The equator is the circumference of the planet. To discover how fast our planet rotates around the imaginary line between these poles (axis), you will need to calculate its circumference. The following activity will show you how you can calculate this by just knowing the diameter of the circle.

Activity: calculating the rotational speed of the planets

Materials: metric tape measure and ruler, pieces of tagboard, pencil compass, calculator

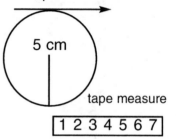

Hold the disk perpendicular to the table and roll it along the tape measure.

- Use the compass to draw three circles with diameters of 5 cm, 8 cm, and 12 cm. Write the size of the diameter on each circle. Cut out each circle and place a line from the center to one edge.

- Place the tape measure on a table. Beginning at the mark on the circle, roll the circle along the tape to find its circumference. Record this data on the chart.

Circumference (measured to nearest mm)	Diameter	= Results
Circle 1 = _____ cm	5 cm	
Circle 2 = _____ cm	8 cm	
Circle 3 = _____ cm	12 cm	
Circle 4 = _____ cm your choice		

- Use this formula to determine Earth's circumference and rotation speed:

  Diameter of Earth _____ miles x 3.14 = _____ miles circumference

  Earth's circumference _____ miles ÷ _____ hours in a day = _____ mph rotation speed

- Add this data to the chart and use this same formula to calculate the rotation of speed of the remaining eight planets.

Rotation Speed of Planets

	Mercury	Venus	Earth	Mars	Jupiter	Saturn	Uranus	Neptune	Pluto
Diameter in Miles	3,050	7,565	7,973	4,246	89,365	75,335	31,948	30,933	1,421
(Kilometers)	(4,880)	(12,104)	(12,756)	(6,794)	(142,984)	(120,536)	(51,118)	(49,492)	(2,274)
Circumference in Miles									
(Kilometers)									
Length of Day (hours)	1416 h	5832 h	24 h	25 h	10 h	11 h	17 h	16 h	153 h
Rotation Speed in mph									
(kph)									

Planet Projects *(cont.)*

Activity: demonstrating how the orbital speed of the planets changes relative to the sun

Materials: plastic drinking straws cut in half, string, rubber washers

- Give each student half a drinking straw, two ft. (60 cm) of string, and two rubber washers.
- Have students assemble the materials in the manner shown below.

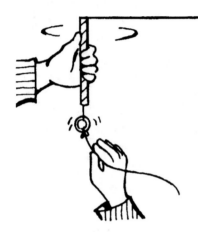

string = sun's gravity

straw = sun

washer = planet

- Have the students stand apart and tell them to hold the straw (as shown). They should begin spinning the string and washer until the string is fully extended. Next, they continue spinning the washer and slowly pull down on the lower washer. The other washer revolves faster and faster as it nears the straw.
- Explain that the straw represents the sun, the string is the sun's gravity, and the washer is a planet. As the planet nears the sun, it revolves faster, thus avoiding being pulled into the sun. List the planets and lengths of their years on the board (see Planetary Facts, page 75).

Activity: showing the phases of Venus

Materials: transparency of Galileos' Proof of a Solar System (page 16), Phases of Venus Flipbook (pages 17 and 18), scissors, glue, unlined file cards, clear packing tape

- Share the information from Controversy of Earth's Position (page 15) to provide background for the transparency of Galileo's Proof of a Solar System.
- Next, tell the students they are going to construct a flipbook from a series of drawings of the phases of Venus as seen through a telescope. Distribute the materials to them and follow the instructions to help them assemble their books.
- When students have finished, tell them to look at the phase and size changes as they flip the pages. Let them discuss why the size of Venus appears to change. (The size changes as it gets closer and then farther from Earth.) Be sure they notice that Venus is largest when it is a thin crescent. The apparent size increase is due to it being so close to Earth during this phase.
- Have students compare the views of Venus with those shown on the transparency of Galileo's Proof of a Solar System.

Controversy of Earth's Position

To the Teacher: Share a summary of the following information with the students when the transparency of Galileo's Proof of a Solar System (page 16) is shown to them.

Early Theories of the Universe

The ancient Greek philosopher Aristotle (350 B.C.) stated the theory that Earth was at the center of the Universe and that the planets, sun, and stars revolved around it. He envisioned a set of 55 celestial spheres, fitting one inside the other. Each of the spheres carried some of the heavenly bodies around Earth. The motions of the spheres combined to explain the various motions of the stars, sun, moon, and planets that observers could see from Earth. Unfortunately, his incorrect theories were taken as fact for nearly 2,000 years, holding back the advancement of science.

In about A.D. 140, the Greek astronomer Ptolemy offered a detailed theory of the universe. His model endorsed Aristotle's theory of a *geocentric* (earth-centered) system. His views were accepted for nearly 1,500 years and were supported by the Catholic Church.

Challengers of the geocentric theory included Copernicus (1473-1543). He thought that if the sun was in the center of the planets, it gave a pleasing and unifying model of the universe and its motions. The telescope was not available yet, so he had no proof of a *heliocentric* (sun-centered) system. His theory was not widely accepted, and he feared the wrath of the Catholic Church since they endorsed the geocentric theory. A book about his theory was published after his death.

Theories of the Universe After the Telescope

When Galileo (1564-1642) first observed and recorded astronomical events through a telescope in late 1609 or early 1610, he discovered that the geocentric theory had to be wrong. With his telescope, he could see the phases of Venus, which are not visible to the unaided eye. He claimed that his observations of the planet's phases proved that it had to be revolving around the sun, not Earth.

Naked eye observations showed that Venus never appeared more than 48° east or west of the sun. Galileo showed that if Venus stayed that close to the sun and revolved around Earth along with the sun, the only phases of Venus visible from Earth would be crescents; and Venus would not change size since it would always be the same distance from Earth.

Galileo's observations showed that the phases of Venus went from a very thin crescent to full and back again. During these phase changes, the size of Venus varied, being larger during the thinnest crescent phases and smallest when it was full. He reasoned these phases and size changes could only happen if Venus and Earth revolved around the sun. Since Venus' orbit is closer to the sun than Earth's orbit, an observer on Earth would never see Venus move very far from the sun.

Galileo got into trouble with the Roman Catholic Church when he wrote a dialogue between two imaginary people—one defending the geocentric system, the other defending the heliocentric system. This was in 1632, the time of the Inquisition, when *heretics* (people who opposed Church teachings) were tortured, imprisoned, and killed. Since Galileo was 68 years old, the Church decided just to place him under house arrest for the remainder of his life. It was not until 1983 that the Church agreed that he was not guilty and should not have been condemned.

Galileo's Proof of a Solar System

Geocentric (Earth-Centered) Model

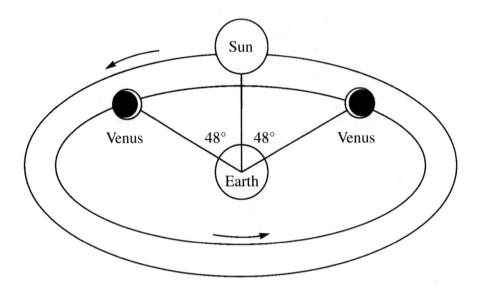

Venus is never seen farther than 48° east or west of the sun. If Venus traveled around Earth, only crescent phases would be visible through a telescope.

Heliocentric (Sun-Centered) Model

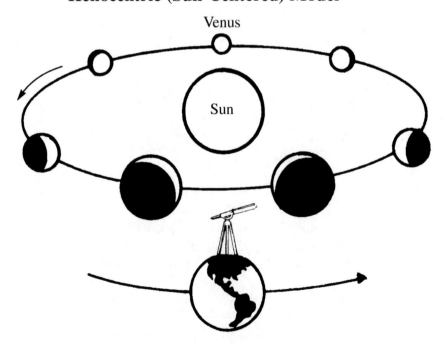

All phases of Venus are visible from Earth through a telescope. The only way this can happen is for Venus to revolve around the sun.

Phases of Venus Flipbook

Instructions

1. Let the students work in small groups. Distribute 18 file cards and a copy of the 18 phases of Venus to each group. Tell them to carefully cut them out and then glue each of these to the lower left corner of a card (see below). Place the cards in order with #1 on top.

2. Stack the cards so the edges are offset about 1/4 in. (.6 cm). Hold them in place with a rubber band.

3. Place a piece of clear packing tape vertically across the back of the cards and over the top edge of the front.

4. Put another piece of tape horizontally across the back of the cards to hold them in place. Be sure this tape does not lock the cards into place in such a way that the phases are not completely visible when the cards are flipped.

5. Have students hold the cards in one hand and flip through them rapidly, looking at the phases of Venus. They should do this several times to see the changes in shape and size.

6. Explain that the phases show the full cycle.

a. single card

b. two cards

c. stacked cards

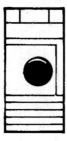

d. flipbook

Phases of Venus Flipbook *(cont.)*

Flipbook Pages

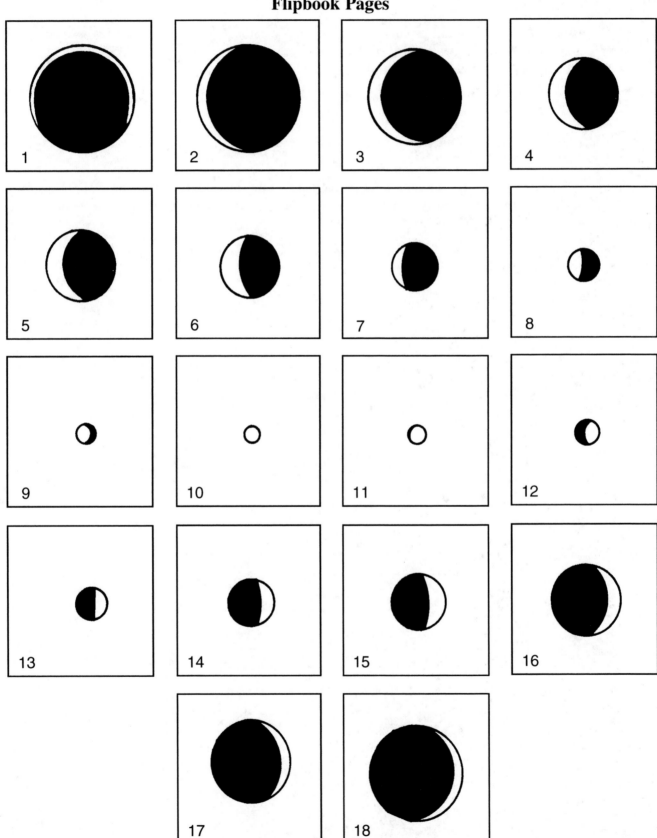

Looking at the Moon

Moon Phases (*The Young Astronomer*, pages 18 and 19; *The Visual Dictionary of the Universe*, pages 36 and 37; *Guide to Space*, page 18)

Show the moon information from *The Young Astronomer*, pointing out the phases. Show students how phases are created by sunlight reflected from the moon (inner circle). Point out how these phases change as seen from Earth during the approximate four-week cycle (outer circle). Point out that the phases switch sides halfway through. For example, the waxing crescent is on the moon's right side just after the new phase. When the moon has moved around Earth about four weeks later, the light of the waning crescent is on the left.

Note: The photograph of the last quarter moon (page 19 of *The Young Astronomer*) shows the phase for a day earlier. The photograph of the first quarter shows the correct quarter moon. The dark portion or *terminator* is a straight line.

Show the pictures illustrating the phases of the moon in the other two books.

Activity: observing the moon

Materials: unlined file cards, rubber bands

- Check a calendar or the newspaper to find the date of the new moon. Begin this activity two days after that date.

- Tell students that, like Galileo and other astronomers, they are going to make astronomical observations. They will observe the moon each evening and draw the shape of its phase. Their records will be made on a different file card each evening.

- Distribute 14 file cards and a rubber band to each student. Have them place a date on each card, beginning with today's date. Give them a time which is 30 minutes after sunset to write on the first card.

- Tell them that they are to take these cards home and go outside each evening, beginning today, where they can get a clear view of the moon. They should make an exact drawing of the moon's shape and the time of their observation.

- Explain that they should repeat observations every evening from the same spot and at the same time. They should record the time of the observation on each card.

- Tell students they are to report the shape of the moon daily and record it on a chart. They are to continue this assignment even during days they are not in school. Their data will be recorded on the classroom chart after they return.

- If the previous evening was too cloudy to record the moon, have students think of a way to fill in the missing data. (Draw the moon when it is next visible and compare it to the last drawing. Fill in the missing shapes that come between these two.)

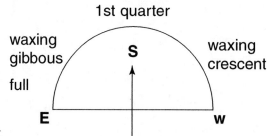

View of moon phases for two weeks. Observations are made about 30 minutes after sunset.

- After three days, ask the students what else is happening besides a change in the phases. (The moon is moving farther east each day, away from the sun.)

Looking at the Moon *(cont.)*

Activity: simulating the phases of the moon

Materials: clamp-on light fixture, 150-watt clear light bulb, three-inch Styrofoam balls and stir sticks or wood skewers, transparency of The Moon's Phases (page 21)

- Conduct this activity after students have observed and recorded moon phases for two weeks. This background is needed to understand the simulation.

- This activity must be done in a darkened room. Clamp the light high above all heads. Distribute a Styrofoam ball and stick to each person. Have each one push a stick into a ball. Tell them the ball represents the moon, their heads represent Earth, their noses represent where they live on the planet, and the lamp is the sun.

- Darken the room after turning on the bright light. Simulate the new moon by holding a ball in front of you to block out the light. Have the students do this and notice that the side of the moon they see does not reflect the light. This phase is the *new moon.* (This is actually a solar eclipse position, but an explanation will appear later.)

- Have students hold the moon in front of them and slowly turn counterclockwise, watching as the "sun's" light falls on the moon. Have them stop when they can see light beginning to show on the ball. Explain that this is a crescent moon, seen after a new phase. Notice the crescent is on the right side of the moon.

- Let students continue to turn slowly, looking for the first quarter, gibbous, and finally the full moon. They must raise the ball overhead so the full moon is not lost in their shadow. Ask them where the sun is at this time. (*on the other side of Earth*)

- As they continue to turn, have them notice that the light is now appearing on the left side of the moon and that the phases go in reverse—from gibbous to quarter to crescent. Repeat this and use the transparency of moon phases to review what students have seen with the moon models.

Activity: learning about moon phases on the Net (assessment for phases of the moon)

Materials: Internet access, copies of The Moon's Phases (page 22)

- Let students visit the following Web site to find and record the moon's phase on various dates.

  Moon's Phases Through Time
  http://www.naturalist.net/Moon_Phases_through_time.htm

- Distribute copies of The Moon's Phases on page 22 to all students and review it with them. Designate times they can visit the Web site to gather their data.

- When all students have completed the assignment, discuss their findings. If needed, help students to answer the question regarding Earth's phase on July 20, 1969. Use the transparency of The Moon's Phases to illustrate this concept.

  1. When looking at Earth from the moon, the phase of Earth would be the opposite of the phase we see of the moon from Earth. For example, if we see a new moon from Earth, Earth itself would be in full phase as seen from the moon.

  2. The moon was a waxing crescent on July 20, 1969. The astronauts would have seen Earth as a waning gibbous. Visit the Web site below and put in the date July 20, 1969. Submit this to see the waning gibbous Earth as it would have appeared to astronauts from the moon.

  Solar System Simulator http://space.jpl.nasa.gov/

The Moon's Phases

Compare the phases of the moon on this chart with those you saw in the simulation.

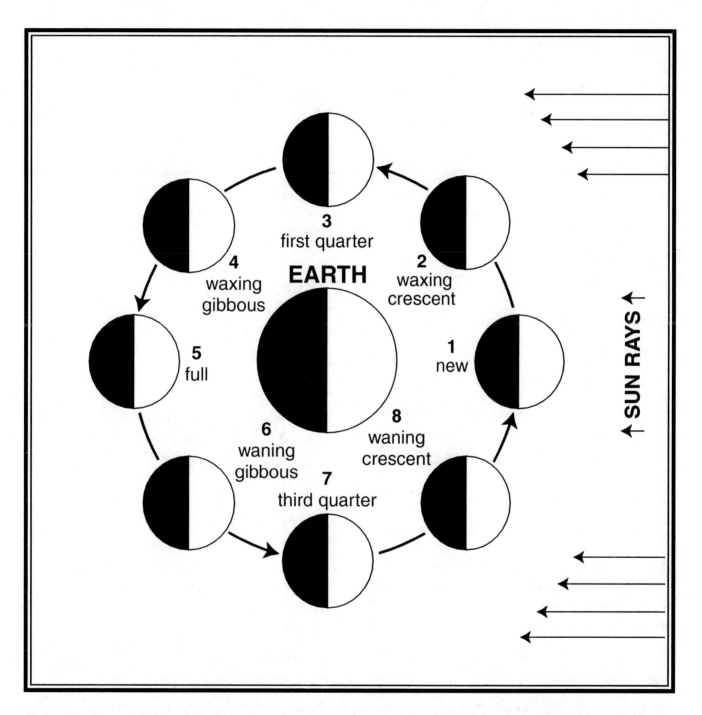

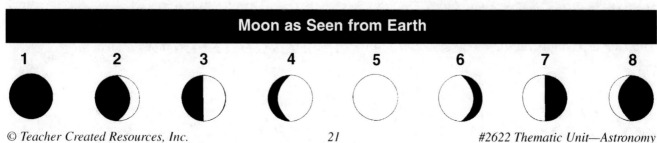

The Moon's Phases *(cont.)*

Instructions: Visit the Web site shown below to discover the phase of the moon on dates specified on the chart, as well as one that you select.

Moon's Phases Through Time

 http://www.naturalist.net/Moon_Phases_through_time.htm

When you reach this site, you will be asked to give the century, year, month, day, time, and time zone settings; then click on "submit" to see the moon's phase. Set the century if needed and leave the time at 0 and time zone at Universal Time.

Find the phase for:	Year	Month	Day	Phase	
				Drawing	**Name of phase**
1. today					
2. your birthday					
3. first landing on the moon	1969	July	20		
4. next full moon					
5. your choice					

Earth goes through phases just as the moon does. When the first astronauts landed on the moon and looked back at Earth, what phase would they see? Think about the simulation you did to see the moon phases using a ball and bright light. Remember the new phase and imagine yourself on the moon looking back at Earth. What would Earth look like?

If I were standing on the moon when it is a new moon, Earth would be in the _____ phase.

This phase is the _____ of the moon's phase as seen from Earth.

(*Hint*: Look at the chart of The Moon's Phases on page 21 to help you with the answer.)

The first astronauts on the moon saw Earth in the _____ phase.

Eclipses

Activity: simulating solar and lunar eclipses

Materials: 150-watt clamp-on lamp, Styrofoam balls, transparency of Eclipses (page 24), *Guide to Space* (pages 10 and 11); *The Young Astronomer* (page 22); *The Visual Dictionary of the Universe* (page 57)

- Let the students resume their positions with the moon balls and lamp to simulate the new moon phase. Point out that when they hold the moon directly in front of their eyes, the sun disappears. The moon is much smaller than the sun, but it appears to be about the same size since it is closer to Earth. When Earth, moon, and sun line up during a new moon phase, the moon covers the sun, creating a solar eclipse.

- If students look at the shadow cast on a neighbor's face, they will see that it is round since the moon is a sphere. Have them stand still and slowly move the moon balls counterclockwise around their heads. As they watch their neighbors' faces, they will see how the shadow sweeps across them. Explain that if you could go into space to see a solar eclipse, you would see Earth with a round shadow sweeping across its surface. The length of the total portion of an eclipse varies from about 1.3 to 7.2 minutes.

- Only people within that circular shadow would see the total eclipse. People near the outer edges would see only part of the sun disappear. Those farther away would not see any eclipse of the sun. This experience can be simulated by raising and lowering the moon ball in front of the light.

- Have the students stand in a *full* moon position, with the sun directly at their backs. Tell them to lower the moon so that their own shadows cut off the light from the sun. This is a *total lunar eclipse*. Lunar eclipses are visible to anyone who can see the moon in the sky while it is being eclipsed by Earth. Total lunar eclipses take hours from beginning to end.

- Use the transparency of Eclipses to give further details about solar and lunar eclipses.

- Explain that solar and lunar eclipses do not occur every time the moon is full or new. The moon's orbit around Earth is tilted so that most of the time it is above or below the sun during new moon and thus does not block the sun. During full moon, the moon's orbit usually carries it above or below Earth; thus, Earth's shadow does not fall on the moon.

- As an assessment of this activity, have each student write a letter home to explain how solar and lunar eclipses occur, including drawings of each of these.

- Show the pictures that illustrate eclipses in the three books.

- Have students look up the next total solar and lunar eclipses on page 57 of *The Visual Dictionary of the Universe*. Show them the world map on page 11 of *Guide to Space*, which illustrates the paths of these solar eclipses to 2020. See if any of these approach where students live now and determine how old they will be when this happens.

Eclipses *(cont.)*

Lunar Eclipse

Umbra · Moon · Penumbra · Earth · Sun · Moon · Earth

Solar Eclipse

The Moon's Path During Full Phase: total eclipse (A); partial eclipses (B & C); no eclipse (D)

C · A · B · D · Penumbra · Umbra

Path of Total Solar Eclipse: August 11, 1999

ends at sunset

Northern limit of partial eclipse

sun 20% eclipsed · 40% · 60% · 80% · 80% · 60% · 40% · 20%

Path of total eclipse

Begins at sunrise

Southern limit of partial eclipse

24

Eclipses *(cont.)*

Activity: examining solar and lunar eclipse pictures on the Net
Materials: Internet access

- On the following Web page, you will find spectacular pictures of solar eclipses, listed in order from top to bottom.

Richard Horwitz Picture Library

http://www.kidseclipse.com/kidseclipse/pages/a3b4c0d0.htm

1. Two pictures of the sun appear hidden by the moon. The one on the left shows more of the sun's corona (outer atmosphere), which extends beyond the sun and can be seen only during an eclipse. The picture on the right shows the inner, brighter, part of the corona and may have been taken using a *coronagraph*, a telescope with a black disk to block out the center of the sun so the brighter part of the corona can be studied.
2. *Baily's beads* (the "diamond ring" effect) show the finals flash of sunlight through a lunar valley on the disappearing crescent of the sun. There are two pictures.
3. Between two Baily's beads pictures is a time-lapse photograph showing the sun gradually disappearing behind the moon until the moon covers the sun except for a bright corona. The sun reappears as the moon continues its orbit around Earth.
4. The moon is just beginning to cover the sun; it appears as if a small bite has been taken from the sun.
5. An *annular solar eclipse* is last. Here the moon is slightly farther from Earth, so it appears to be smaller than the sun's image. In this eclipse the outer edge of the sun is still visible, much as if a cannon ball had just been fired through the sun.

- The April 3–4, 1996, and September 27, 1996, lunar eclipses appear at the following Web site. This is a series of pictures from first contact with Earth's *penumbra* (outer shadow) to the moon within the *umbra* (darkest shadow) and finally reemerging.

Lunar Eclipse Images

http://www.geocities.com/CapeCanaveral/5993/

Activity: making models of the moon
Materials: large Styrofoam ball, gray construction paper, pencil compass

- Use page 37 of *The Visual Dictionary of the Universe*, which shows cutaway views of the moon. Have a student make a model of this from the Styrofoam ball to add to those made in an earlier activity for each of the planets.
- Have a paper model of the moon made which can be added to the set made in the planet scale models earlier. The moon is 2,160 miles (3,476 km) in diameter. Using the scale of Earth's radius of 7,973 miles (12,756 km) being equal to 5 cm, the radius for the scale model for the moon would be 1.4 cm.
- See page 20 of *The Young Astronomer* for models of the lunar surface.

Activity: learning about the moon on the Net
Materials: transparency and copies of The Moon on the Net (pages 26 and 27)

- Distribute copies of The Moon on the Net and have students follow the instructions to get information about the moon. Divide them into groups and assign pairs to research different sections of the worksheets.

The Moon

http://www.solarviews.com/eng/moon.htm#intro
Keyword: Moon

- When groups complete this assignment, have them share what they learn.

The Moon on the Net

Instructions: Visit the Web site shown below. Scan down the list of information and click on *The Moon Introduction*. Read this information and find answers to the following questions. Write the answers on another piece of paper or the back of this page.

The Moon

http://www.solarviews.com/eng/moon.htm

Moon Introduction

1. When we look at the moon, what can we see without a telescope?

2. When Galileo and others looked at the moon with telescopes, what did they see?

3. Is the moon more or less dense than Earth?

4. Who was the first person to walk on the moon, and when did this take place?

5. How did the astronauts communicate with each other and people back on Earth?

6. If a person had been standing on the moon during the landing, would he or she have been able to hear anything? Explain your answer.

7. Explain what it would look like as you stand on the moon and then move around.

8. From Earth, we can see only one side of the moon. Explain why.

9. How do we know what the interior of the moon is like?

10. Are there any moonquakes?

11. How does the crust of the moon compare to the crust of Earth?

12. Is the core of the moon like that of Earth?

13. How old is the moon, and how do we know?

14. Is the moon still being impacted by large meteors?

The Moon on the Net *(cont.)*

Instructions: Visit the Web site below and click on *Moon Introduction*. Scan down to *Views of the Moon*. Read the description for each of the pictures listed below. On another piece of paper or on the back of this page write the information requested.

The Moon

http://www.solarviews.com/eng/moon.htm

Views of the Moon

1. **The Lunar Interior:** Tell about the moon's layers.

2. *Apollo 17:* (Whole Moon View) Describe what the astronauts on this mission saw.

3. **Moon—False Color Mosaic:** The orbiting unmanned Galileo spacecraft photographed the moon's surface in December 1992. It used special filters, which highlighted various features on the surface. Tell what the colors showed.

4. **Far Side of the Moon:** We never see the far side of the moon. It was first photographed by the Soviet Union in the early 60s, and later by the *Apollo 11* crew. Describe what they saw. Why is this side different from the side facing Earth?

5. **Lunar South Pole:** This mosaic picture of the moon's south polar region was made from 1,500 images taken from *Clementine,* an unmanned spacecraft orbiting the moon. Summarize what the pictures tell us about this area.

6. *Apollo 11:* Look at each of the four pictures and read the captions. Click on the picture showing Earth from the moon. When you reach this Web page, click on *earthris gif* to see an enlarged view of this image. What is Earth's phase in this picture? Does this confirm the answer to he last question asked about Earth's phase on The Moon's Phase data sheet (page 22)?

7. *Apollo 15:* Click on this picture and then click on *rover gif* at this new Web page to see an enlarged picture of the rover. Describe what it looks like and what you see on the ground. Why are there fenders over the wheels?

8. *Apollo 17:* Look at the first three pictures and read the captions. What color is the sky? Find the picture which shows Earth above the huge rock, and click on that picture. When you get to the new Web page, click on the *boulder gif.* What is the phase of earth in this picture? What moon phase would we see from Earth at the same time?

9. *Apollo 17:* Describe the orange soil the astronauts found.

Man on the Moon

Activity: reviewing the *Apollo* moon landings
Materials: *The Visual Dictionary of the Universe* (pages 54 and 55); *Guide to Space* (pages 20 and 21)
Internet access

- Show students the pictures and information from the books regarding the Soviet exploration of the moon by satellite and unmanned landings before *Apollo 11* and the *Apollo* lunar landings.
- Have students visit the following Web site to learn about the competition between the Soviet Union and United States to be the first to put a man on the moon. It also contains detailed information regarding *Apollo* missions, which went to the moon.

The Moon
http://www.solarviews.com/eng/moon.htm#views

- Beginning at the top of this Web page, scan down to Apollo Landing Missions.
- Divide the students into groups to gather information from the following sections under this topic. The size of the groups should vary since the amount of information in each section varies. The information about *Apollo* missions is lengthy, and these might be divided between two students per mission. Links to pictures and animations are offered at these sites. Some of the graphics in these require large amounts of memory space and will take time and sometimes special software to download.
   1. Prologue
   2. Spacecraft, Suits, and Rovers
   3. Precursors to the Landing Missions
   4. *Apollo 11, Apollo 12, Apollo 13, Apollo 14, Apollo 15, Apollo 16, Apollo 17*
   5. Epilogue: When might we go back to the moon?
- Have each group prepare a report for the class. Encourage them to show some of the pictures from Web pages they used.

   More information about the history of space exploration is available at the following links:

History of Space Exploration
http://www.solarviews.com/eng/history.htm

NASA Search Site
http://www.nasa.gov/search/
Keyword: Space Exploration

Activity: learning what causes the tides
Materials: *The Young Astronomer* (page 24); transparency of Explanation of the Tides (pages 29 and 30); (Optional: Internet access)

- In *The Young Astronomer,* show the students the information in which briefly introduces the tides. Do the activity outlined on this page (24), using magnets to demonstrate a force field with properties similar to gravity. Be sure the students understand that gravity does not have a repelling force as magnets do.
- Show the transparency of the Explanation of the Tides to provide information on how the moon and sun pull on the ocean and Earth to create tides.

   If Internet access is available, let students visit the following Web site to read an explanation of the tides and see graphics which illustrate these.

Lunar Tides
http://csep10.phys.utk.edu/astr161/lect/time/tides.html

Explanation of the Tides

Tides in the ocean are caused mostly by the pull of the moon on Earth. The moon's gravity pulls up water which is directly beneath it, creating a high tide there. Another high tide occurs on the other side of Earth since the moon pulls the solid Earth away from the water. As Earth turns, high tide occurs at each place on the ocean twice a day.

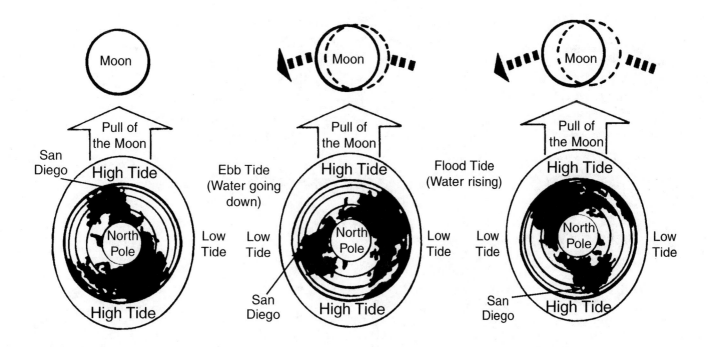

High tide occurs directly below the moon and on the opposite side of Earth. When Earth is in the position (above), San Diego has a high tide.

As Earth turns, the tides rise and fall all along coastlines. About 6 hours and 13 minutes after a high tide, San Diego has a low tide (above).

The next high tide at San Diego is about 12 hours and 25 minutes after the first.

Explanation of the Tides *(cont.)*

Spring Tides

Spring tides are extremely high and extremely low. This is created when the sun and moon pull together. These occur twice each month near the full and new moons.

Neap Tides

Neap tides do not rise as high nor fall as low as normal tides. They occur twice a month when the moon is near its first and last quarters and are caused by the moon and sun pulling at a right angle.

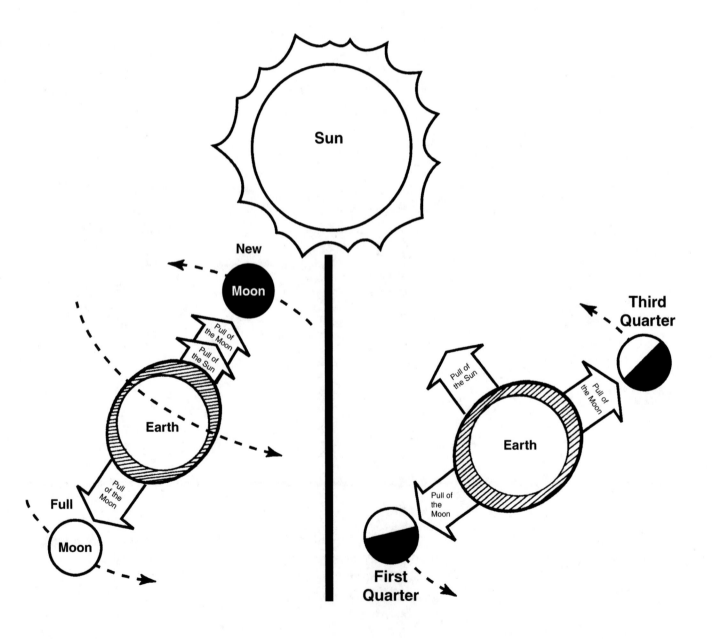

Spots on the Sun

What Are Sunspots? (*The Visual Dictionary of the Universe,* pages 28 and 29; *The Young Astronomer,* pages 22 and 23; and *Guide to Space,* pages 8 and 9)

Share the information regarding the sun provided in these books. Do the activity to show what happens when the sun's energy is concentrated with a magnifying glass (*The Young Astronomer,* page 23). The activity on pages 22 and 23 of this book shows how to project and record sunspots. The activity described below provides further information about projecting the sun's image. Both telescopes and binoculars need to be supported on a tripod or other device during the time it takes to observe and record the sunspots.

Background

Chinese astronomers reported seeing dark spots on the sun in the 1400s. They most likely saw this when the sun was covered by fog, thin clouds, or at sunset. The sunspots they observed must have been very large to be visible without a telescope.

Galileo observed sunspots in the early 1600s when he projected the sun's image through a telescope. Most people then believed the sun was an unchanging celestial object. He saw this was not true since the sunspots moved across the sun, changing shape and size.

Observations of sunspots over the centuries revealed some systematic behavior. The number of spots varies, reaching a peak about every 11 years. Between peak numbers of spots, their locations on the sun change steadily from middle latitudes to concentration near the equator. At the beginning of a cycle when the sunspot number is maximized, most of them appear in activity bands about 30° north or south of the sun's equator. During the next 11 years, the spots tend to lie ever closer to the equator, and by the end of the cycle they are nearly on it. Sunspots at the equator take 25.04 days to move once around the sun while those on the rest of the sun take about 28 days. This rotation can be detected by observing the motion of sunspots on the sun's surface.

A hint of the origin of the spots was found when their magnetic properties were measured in the first decade of this century. The magnetic field was found to be especially intense in sunspots, about 1,000 times stronger than the surrounding areas of the sun. The sun is a star made mostly of heated helium (25%) and hydrogen (73%) gases. It is now thought that the intense magnetic field in the sunspot area inhibits convection, so that heated gas from below cannot rise up to the surface. Thus, the spot is cooler than its surroundings and therefore is not as bright. A typical sunspot may have a diameter of 20,000 miles or 32,000 km (Earth's diameter is 7,973 miles or 12,757 km).

When *magnetograms* (maps of magnetic field strength) were made of sunspots, they were found to act like north or south magnetic poles. Pairs of spots often appear together, the two members of a pair usually having opposite magnetic polarities.

Sunspot groups are the scenes of the most violent solar activity, the *solar flare*. These gigantic outbursts of charged particles result from extremely hot gas spouting upward from the surface. Flares are most common when the greatest number of spots is seen on the solar surface. Charged particles flow outward from a flare. Some of them escape into the solar wind and may hit Earth. Earth is bathed by an extra dosage of solar wind particles some three days after a flare, creating effects on radio communications and brilliant displays of the aurora. This happened on August 7, 1972, when one of the largest flares led to power blackouts, short-wave radio blackouts, and auroras extending far from the Arctic and Antarctic Circles.

Spots on the Sun *(cont.)*

Activity: viewing and recording sunspots (an activity requiring several weeks)

Materials: telescope or binoculars, white paper, cardboard box, piece of cardboard about 1 ft. (30 cm) square, Daily Sunspot Record (page 34), Analyzing the Sunspot Records (page 35), the three reference books, (*Optional:* Internet access)

- Have students make observations of the sun using a telescope or binoculars (see preparation on page 33). Label each day's data with the date and time recorded. Post the data on a bulletin board so students can see daily changes.
- After collecting at least five days of data through the telescope, have the students visit the Big Bear Solar Observatory (BBSO) Web site shown below.

  Big Bear Solar Observatory Latest Images
  http://www.bbso.njit.edu/cgi-bin/LatestImages
- This observatory provides current solar images. Look for the white-light image and click on halfsize image. Print this, adding date and time. Distribute copies of the Daily Sunspot Record; let students copy each day's record and compare data.
- At the Web site, scan down to "High Resolution Observations" to find the white image close-up of sunspots. Click on it and print a copy. The *umbra* (dark inner region) and *penumbra* (lighter outer shadow around the umbra) will be visible. So will the odd shapes of the spots. Explain that sunspots are usually much larger than Earth.
- Distribute a copy of Analyzing the Sunspot Record after four days of data have been gathered. Have students continue to record the data for five more days, describing what they see (changes in the size, shape, number, and location of sunspots).
- It will be seen that sunspots move gradually across the sun, disappearing around the other side (new spots may also appear from the other side). By observing this, scientists like Galileo could determine that the sun rotated in about 28 days.
- Since the sun is not solid but made of gases, the center (equator) rotates more rapidly than the poles. Ask students what happens in a race between sunspots at the equator and those at the poles. (*The equator wins.*) Have them look for this in their data.
- Let students compare the H-Alpha Image at the BBSO Web site to the pictures in *Guide to Space* (page 9). The H-Alpha Image also shows arches of solar flares leaping from the sun.
- Current colored pictures of the sun's surface can be found at the Web site below of an Australian observatory.

  Learmonth Solar Images H-Alpha
  http://www.ips.gov.au/learmonth/solar/index.htmI

Assessment

- Print out another series of five days of solar images from the Internet, but do not let the students see them. Show the date on the first image but hide the other four on the backs of the pictures. Assign a letter to each of the images. Arrange them on a bulletin board with the first image in the line and all the others out of sequence.
- Let the students suggest the correct sequence, and then write a brief summary of how they came to the conclusion.
- Have students draw circles for the sun, showing where they think sunspots would be the next day. Show the print of the next day's data to compare with their predictions. Tell them to write an illustrated summary of what was learned.

Spots on the Sun *(cont.)*

Lesson Preparation

Tape the paper into the bottom of the box. Set the box on an easel or chair so it can be moved into position to capture the sun's image. Cut a hole in the cardboard so that it fits snugly around the tube on the telescope or binoculars. Be sure the sun is passing through the objective lens of the binoculars and then the eyepiece to the paper. It is incorrectly shown in the *Young Astronomer* book.

Never Look Directly at the Sun; It Can Cause Blindness!

Focus the instrument on the most distant object you can find. If binoculars are used, cover one lens. Set up the telescope or binoculars so that the image of the sun can be projected into the box and will shine on the white cardboard. Some adjustments will need to be made once the sun's image is projected into the box so that it can be focused.

Use a steady tripod for telescope or binoculars. Project the sun's image by aiming the telescope or binoculars in the general direction of the sun WITHOUT LOOKING THROUGH THE INSTRUMENT. This is done, by watching the shadow cast by the telescope or binoculars as you move it into position. When the shadow of the optical instrument is as small as it can get and a bright circle appears on the ground, the instrument is pointing at the sun. Move the box so that this image falls on the paper. Place the cardboard around the lens to cast a shadow around the bright image of the sun, thus making it easier to see on the paper. Focus the image until the edge of the sun appears sharp. Sketch in the circle made by the sun's image and mark the top of the circle with the word "top." Sunspots will appear as dark spots within the bright image. Unlike dirt on the lens, they will move with the sun as it drifts out of view of the lens. Use a pencil to draw the sunspots on the paper. (*Note:* Due to Earth's rapid rotation, the sun's image will move out of the lens, so constant adjustment will be needed.) Remove the paper and use a compass to draw the circle. Cut out the circle, record the date and time, and then post it. Cut additional circles of white paper the same size for future data.

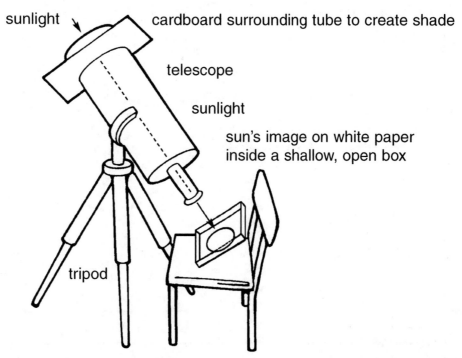

sunlight — cardboard surrounding tube to create shade

telescope

sunlight

sun's image on white paper inside a shallow, open box

tripod

Spots on the Sun *(cont.)*

Daily Sunspot Record

Within the circles below, carefully draw the shape, size, and location of the sunspots you observed daily. Note the date and time under each of them. Compare pairs of sunspot data and write your

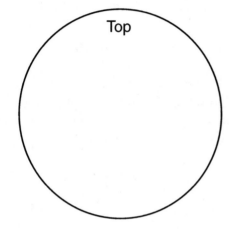

Date: _____

Time: _____

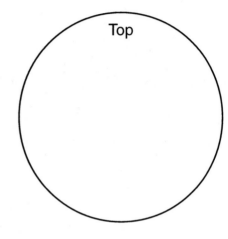

Date: _____

Time: _____

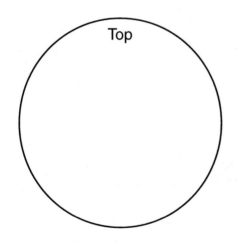

Date: _____

Time: _____

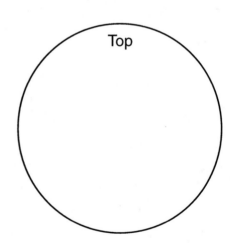

Date: _____

Time: _____

Spots on the Sun *(cont.)*

Analyzing the Sunspot Records

1. Collect five more days of sunspot data and record it below.

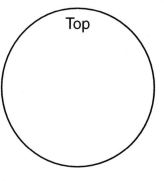

Date: _____

Time: _____

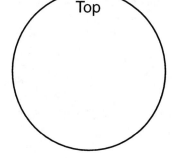

Date: _____

Time: _____

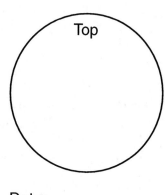

Date: _____

Time: _____

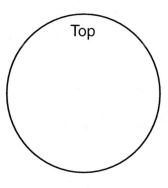

Date: _____

Time: _____

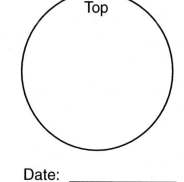

Date: _____

Time: _____

2. Look carefully at this sunspot data and the previous four days of data. If pictures of sunspot activity for these dates were collected from the Internet, include them in your analysis to provide more information. Describe what you see happening to the sunspots over this time period.

_____

_____

3. I predict that when I next observe the sun, the sunspots will be in the locations shown in my drawing to the right because

_____

_____

_____

_____

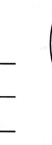

Date: _____

The Geomagnetic Field

Activity: simulating the geomagnetic field

Materials: globe or map showing the geomagnetic poles, circle and bar magnets (See Resource section), iron filings, jar, piece of nylon stocking, rubber band, glass pie-plate, overhead projector, transparency of Earth's Poles and Earth's Magnetic Tail (page 37)

Background

Although the magnetic field is invisible, it can be made visible by outlining it with iron filings. If the filings are sprinkled directly onto a magnet, they will cling to it. However, if something such as paper or glass is laid over the magnet and then the iron filings are sprinkled over the magnet, they spread out along the magnetic field. This demonstration is an excellent way to show what the geomagnetic field looks like.

Classroom Activity

- Distribute magnets to the students and let them play with them to discover their magnetic fields.

- Explain that Earth is surrounded by a strong magnetic field caused by its core. This field is called the *geomagnetic field.*

- Ask the students if they can feel the magnetic field around their magnets when two are brought together. *(Yes, magnets either attract or repel each other and don't need to touch for this reaction to take place.)*

- Ask the students if they can see this field. *(No, it is an invisible force surrounding the magnet.)*

- Explain that you are going to do a demonstration that shows what this field looks like.

Demonstration

- Place a bar magnet in the center of the stage of an overhead projector. Cover it with the glass pie-plate.

- Explain that you are going to outline the magnetic field of the bar magnet, using iron filings. Tell students the glass will prevent filings from sticking to the magnet.

- Pour about two tablespoons (30 mL) of iron filings into the jar. Cover the top with a piece of stocking and hold it in place with the rubber band.

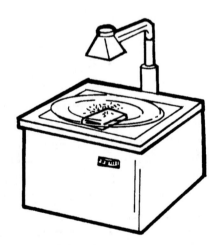

- Gently shake the iron filings over the surface of the bar magnet. It should look like the drawing.

- Explain that the geomagnetic field of Earth would look just like this pattern if we could somehow cover it with glass and sprinkle iron filings over the glass. Like the bar magnet, the geomagnetic field has a north and south pole, with magnetism concentrated at the poles. Magnetism flows between the poles in an arc as seen in the iron filing demonstration.

- Use the transparency to review the geomagnetic poles and field around Earth. Point out the Van Allen Belts, which are like the pattern of iron filings outlining the magnetic field. The belts dip (*converge*) at the geomagnetic poles.

- On a globe or atlas, show students where the geomagnetic poles are located.

The Geomagnetic Field *(cont.)*

Earth's Poles

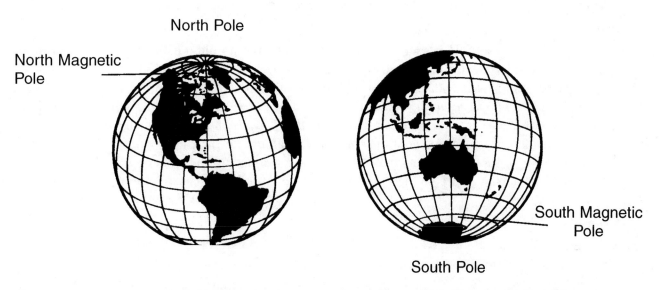

North Pole

North Magnetic Pole

South Magnetic Pole

South Pole

The geographic North and South Poles are at the ends of the axis around which Earth spins. The geomagnetic poles are inclined at an angle of about 11.5° from these North and South Poles. The North geomagnetic pole is near Ellef Ringnes Island, Canada, about 870 miles (1,392 km) from the North Pole. The South geomagnetic pole is off the coast of Wilkes Land in Antarctica and is about 1,710 miles (2,736 km) from the South Pole. The geomagnetic poles move over time.

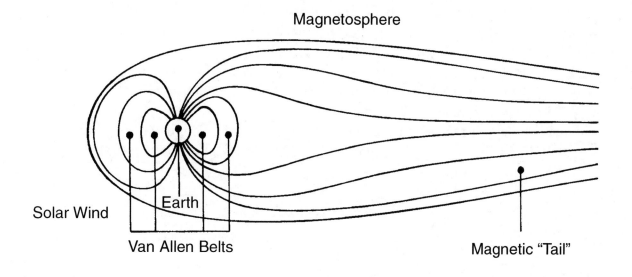

Magnetosphere

Solar Wind

Earth

Van Allen Belts

Magnetic "Tail"

Earth's Magnetic Tail

The magnetism around Earth is called the *magnetosphere*. Radiation from the sun (*solar wind*) blows the magnetosphere into a long tail. An area which consists of large numbers of electrons and protons from the sun is trapped by the magnetism in the *Van Allen Belts*. The aurora occurs in this area 60-620 miles (97-1,000 kilometers) above Earth.

The Aurora

Activity: learning about the aurora

Materials: pictures of the aurora, Internet access, Aurora Research Cards (pages 38 and 39), transparency of Earth's Poles and Earth's Magnetic Tail (page 37), *Guide to Space* (pages 27 and 30)

Background

The *aurora borealis* (northern lights) and *aurora australis* (southern lights) have been sources of myth since ancient times. These beautiful phenomena appear as thin veils of colored light, usually green, moving silently across the sky. Today, we know they result from disturbances in the magnetic field surrounding Earth (*geomagnetic field*). The disturbances are caused by interaction with the *solar wind*, a continuous flow of electrically charged particles from the sun. When there are many sunspots on the sun, increased particles are released and, thus, there is a brighter aurora. The aurora is usually visible only from latitudes near the geomagnetic poles but may be seen nearer the equator during times of peak sunspot activity. The aurora occurs in the upper atmosphere, usually 60-620 miles (97-1,000 km) above Earth.

Classroom Activity

- Use the transparency Earth's Magnetic Tail to review information learned in the previous lesson. Show the students pictures of aurora of Jupiter and Saturn from *Guide to Space*.

- Visit the Web site below as an introduction to the students. Explain that when people first saw these beautiful displays in the sky, they were afraid. Not knowing what caused them, they made up stories to explain these phenomena. Tour the spectacular photos and read the information on pages 1–4. If possible, use a large monitor to show the details.

  The Aurora

  http://gedds.pfrr.alaska.edu/aurora/english/introl.htm

- Tell students that they will visit a variety of Web sites to learn more. One site comes from the University of Alaska, near the North Geomagnetic Pole. Show where Fairbanks is located relative to the North Geomagnetic Pole.

- Divide students into groups and give each a research card. Assign more students to the starred cards since they require a longer time to complete. Review the assignments and set a time to complete the research and prepare a presentation for the class.

- Before presenting their information in the order of the cards, have each group meet with those presenting before and after them to coordinate and avoid repeating information provided by another group.

Assessment

Have students write their own illustrated legend to explain the aurora and then add a summary of the scientific explanation they have learned.

Extender

- Show the students the nine pages of aurora pictures at the following Web site.

  Aurora Images

  http://www.geo.mtu.edu/weather/aurora/images/aurora/jan.curtis/

- Let students see the paintings of Canadian artist Glen Scrimshaw which were inspired by photographs of aurora. Have the students create their own aurora pictures.

  Northern Lights Newest Images

  http://climate.gi.alaska.edu/Curtis/aurora/aurora.html#NEWESTIMAGES

Aurora Research Cards

Aurora Legends

To the Team: You are a team of astronomers who have been asked to be part of a group of scientists who will explain the aurora to a class of students. The information your team is to report is located at a Web site in Fairbanks, Alaska.

- Go to the Web site: http://gedds.pfrr.alaska.edu/aurora/english/Legend1.htm

- Read the information on pages 5-8 and take notes. If possible, make prints of the pictures to use these in your presentation. Set the printer to the horizontal position to keep the pictures from overlapping.

- Prepare your report, including interesting information, pictures from the Web site, or your own drawings to make your presentation exciting.

The Aurora and Polar Explorers

To the Team: You are a team of astronomers who have been asked to be part of a group of scientists who will explain the aurora to a class of students. The information your team is to report is located at a Web site in Fairbanks, Alaska.

- Go to the Web site: http://gedds.pfrr.alaska.edu/aurora/english/Explor1.htm

- Read the information on pages 9-13 and take notes. If possible, make prints of the pictures to use in your presentation. Set the printer to the horizontal position to keep the pictures from overlapping.

- Prepare your report, including interesting information, pictures from the Web site, or your own drawings to make your presentation exciting.

☆ How High in the Sky Are the Aurora?
Where on Earth Can You See the Aurora?

To the Team: You are a team of astronomers who have been asked to be part of a group of scientists who will explain the aurora to a class of students. The information your team is to report is located at a Web site in Fairbanks, Alaska.

- Gather your information from two Web sites listed below.

  How High: http://gedds.pfrr.alaska.edu/aurora/english/Height1.htm (pages 14 and 15)

  Where on Earth: http://gedds.pfr.ralaska.edu/aurora/english/Where1.htm (pages 16-21)

- Read the information and take notes. If possible, make prints of the pictures to use in your presentation. Set the printer to the horizontal position to keep the pictures from overlapping.

- Prepare your report, including interesting information, pictures from the Web site, or your own drawings to make your presentation exciting.

Aurora Research Cards *(cont.)*

✫ Space Weather and Predicting Answers

To the Team: You are a team of astronomers who have been asked to be part of a group of scientists who will explain the aurora to a class of students. The information will come from two Web sites shown below.

- Go to the Web site: http://rigel.rice.edu/~freeman/dmb/spwea.html Read the information and write a brief summary. If possible, print the pictures.

- Go to:http://www.exploratorium.edu/learning_studio/auroras/difcolors.html Current information and predictions of aurora sightings are given here.

  Click on Custom Maps and then click on your location. A map of the North American continent will appear, showing the range predicted for viewing the aurora.

- Prepare your report, including interesting information, pictures from the Web site, or your own drawings to make your presentation exciting.

✫ Aurora Light

To the Team: You are a team of astronomers who have been asked to be part of a group of scientists who will explain the aurora to a class of students. The information your team is to reportis located at the following Web sites.

- **What Kind of Light Does the Aurora Emit?**
  http://gedds.pfrr.alaska.edu/aurora/english/Light1.htm (pages 22-24)

- **What Makes Aurora Happen?**

- http: //www. exploratorium.edu/learning_studio/auroras/happen.html

- **How Is the Aurora Discharge Powered?**

- http://gedds.pfrr.alaska.edu/aurora/english/Powerl.htm (pages 25-29)

- **Why Are They Different Colors?**
  http://www.exploratorium.edu/learning_studio/auroras/difcolors.html

- Prepare your report, including interesting information, pictures from the Web site, or your own drawings to make your presentation exciting.

✫ Aurora Motion and the Sun?

To the Team: You are a team of astronomers who have been asked to be part of a group of scientists who will explain the aurora to a class of students. The information your team is to report is located at the following Web sites.

- **Why Does the Aurora Move?**
  http://gedds.pfrr.alaska.edu/aurora/english/Motion1.htm (pages 30-32)

- **How Does the Sun Affect the Aurora?**
  http://gedds/pfrr.alaska.edu/aurora/english/Sun1.htm (pages 33-39)

- Prepare your report, including interesting information, pictures from the Web site, or your owndrawings to make your presentation exciting.

Sunspots and Magnetic Disturbances on Earth

Activity: finding the relationship between sunspots and magnetic disturbances on Earth

Materials: transparencies and copies of activity sheet (page 42) and graph (page 43), transparencies of the Annual Sunspot Numbers: 1870-1980 graph (page 44) for student groups

Background

Magnetic disturbances affect Earth's upper atmosphere, disrupting communications and creating the aurora. Scientists wondered if there was a correlation between solar activity (sunspots) and magnetic disturbances. Data showing the annual numbers of sunspots beginning in 1870 and those which show the highs and lows of magnetic disturbances on Earth since 1868 indicate that there definitely is a correlation.

The launch of *Explorer I* satellite into Earth orbit in 1958 was part of the International Geophysical Year (IGY). The data from this satellite helped to answer the questions of how changes in sunspot numbers cause the aurora and affect the geomagnetic field.

Students will analyze and compare the graphs of sunspot activity and magnetic disturbance so they will be able to see how scientists use this data, collected over many years, to prove the correlation.

Classroom Activity

- Review the information students have studied about sunspots in the previous lesson.

- Divide the students into small groups and distribute copies of the following to them:

    1. Yearly Index of Magnetic Disturbance: 1868-1987 (page 43)

    2. Sunspots and Magnetic Disturbances on Earth activity sheet (page 42)

- Discuss the instructions for the activity sheet. When the students have completed the activity sheet, discuss the results with them. (See Answer Key, page 80.)

- Distribute a printed copy and transparency of the graph Annual Sunspot Numbers: 1870-1980 (page 44) to each group. Have them follow the instructions to compare this graph with the magnetic disturbance graph.

- Use transparencies of the two graphs to discuss what students have discovered from each. Discuss a comparison of these graphs. (See Answer Key, page 80.)

Sunspots and Magnetic Disturbances on Earth *(cont.)*

To the Team: Your science team has been asked to see if there is any connection between the sunspot cycle and the number of magnetic disturbances on Earth. First, examine the graph Yearly Index of Magnetic Disturbance (page 43), which is based on data gathered between 1868 and 1987.

- This graph shows the patterns of high and low occurrences of magnetic disturbances on Earth from 1868 to 1987. The graph is divided into 10-year spans.

- Each bar is one year. For example, look at 1860-1870. The data for this 10-year period is incomplete; only the last two years are shown. The first bar is 1868; the second is 1869.

- The height of each bar indicates the number of magnetic disturbances for that year. The higher the bar, the greater the number of magnetic disturbances.

- Find the nine specific years that show the least magnetic disturbances, following 1879. Record their dates on the chart.

- As you record each year, calculate the number of years between it and the previous time of few disturbances. This is the period between the low-disturbance years. Record the period of years on the chart.

Years of Least Magnetic Disturbance	
Year	**Period Between Years**
Begin: __1879__	
1. __1891__	__12__
2. _____	_____
3. _____	_____
4. _____	_____
5. _____	_____
6. _____	_____
7. _____	_____
8. _____	_____
9. _____	_____
	Total _____

$$\underline{\hspace{2cm}} \div 9 = \underline{\hspace{2cm}}$$

Total Years	Total Period	Average Period Between Years

- The years 1879 and 1891 have been done for you as an example.

  1. What did this data show?

  2. Compare the pattern of low and high occurrences between 1868 and 1930 with 1930 and 1987. What is the trend you see here?

Sunspots and Magnetic Disturbances on Earth *(cont.)*

Yearly Index of Magnetic Disturbances

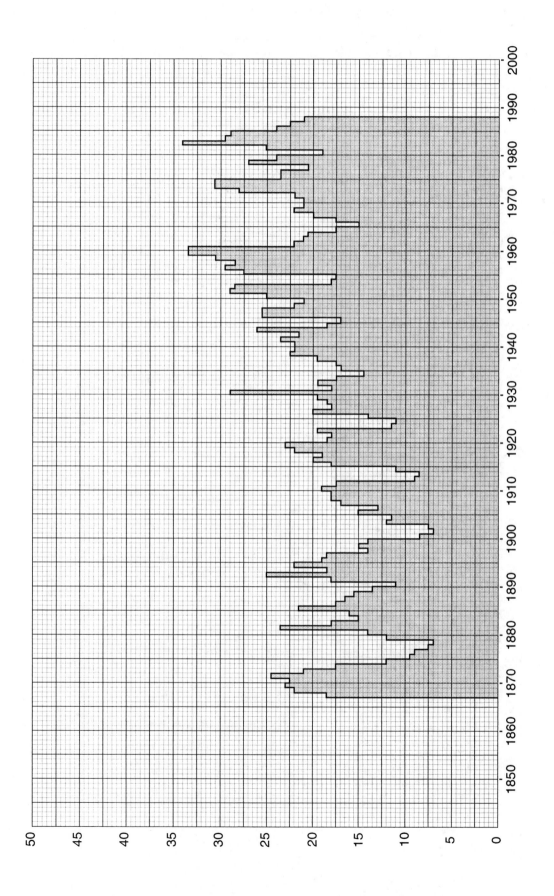

Sunspots and Magnetic Disturbances on Earth *(cont.)*

Annual Sunspot Numbers: 1870-1980

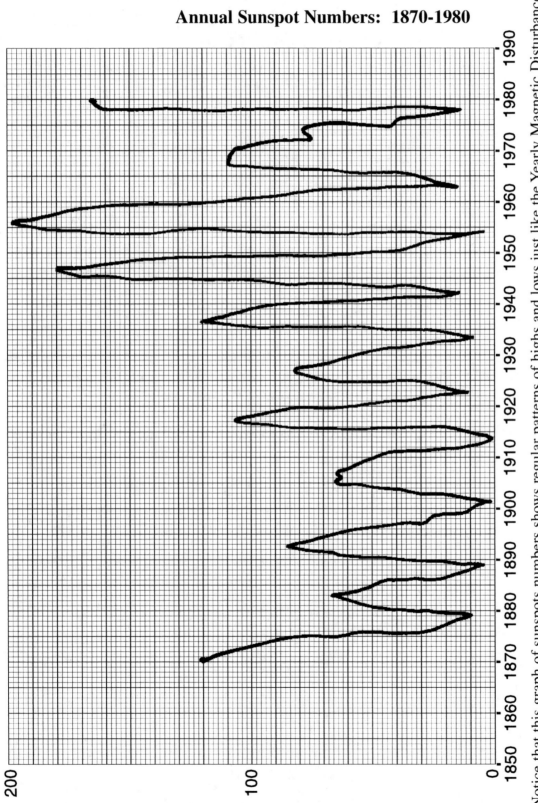

Notice that this graph of sunspots numbers shows regular patterns of highs and lows just like the Yearly Magnetic Disturbance graph. Place the transparency of the Annual Sunspot Numbers: 1870-1980 (page 43) over the Yearly Index of Magnetic Disturbances: 1868-1987 (page 44). Line up the base and date lines of both graphs, matching them from 1870 to 1980. Disregard the different scales for the graphs. Compare the lows for each year of the data on both graphs to see if these show a correlation. Is there a correlation between the number of sunspots and low magnetic disturbances? Explain what this data tells you.

Comets

Dirty Snowballs (*The Visual Dictionary of the Universe,* pages 48 and 49; *The Young Astronomer,* pages 3 and 33; *Guide to Space,* pages 38 and 39)

Excellent introductory information and activities regarding comets are available in these books. Have the students make a comet using the directions in *The Young Astronomer*.

Background

Astronomer Dr. Fred Whipple called comets "dirty snowballs" because of their appearance and content. In fact, the nucleus, or core, of a comet does resemble a large snowball. The core can be from 1/2 to 32 miles (1-56 km) long and is made of small particles, gravel, or large boulders embedded in frozen gases. Comets are not spherical but odd shaped and loosely packed since they have too little mass, and therefore insufficient gravity, to form a sphere.

When a comet travels close to the sun, the ice heats up and some turns into gas. The sun's radiation makes the gas glow, creating the *coma* around the core. Two tails stretch from the comet when near the sun. One tail is dust falling away as it melts. The other tail is gas pushed away by solar wind. These can stretch millions of miles into space and always point away from the sun, even when the comet is headed away from the sun. At that point, the tail would precede the comet as it travels along its orbit.

Until the 17th century, people were not sure what caused comets, nor were they aware that some returned many years later. The astronomer Edmund Halley realized that comets travel in orbits. He recognized a comet he observed in 1682 as one that had appeared in astronomical records 76 years before. He worked out the orbit for the comet, and predicted it would return in 1758. When it did, it was named for him. It still returns about every 76 years, and new comets are continually being discovered.

Demonstration: simulating a comet

Materials: Let's Make a Comet (page 46); Comets on the Net, Parts 1 and 2 (pages 47 and 48)

- Remind students of the model to demonstrate orbital speed of planets around the sun (page 14). This device also shows how comets move around the sun. When a comet is far from the sun, it moves slowly in its orbit, pulled along by the sun's gravity. As the comet gets closer to the sun, its speed increases until it gets close enough to use the sun's gravity to whip around it. The comet then travels along its orbit away from the sun and back into space. Depending upon the orbit, it may return in a few years or millions of years or disappear into space and never be seen again.

- Follow Let's Make a Comet to simulate a comet. Make a transparency of the instructions to use during the construction and a copy to send home with students.

- Have students give the comet a name and place it where all can see it through the day. Take time periodically to examine changes, It will gradually fall apart as the frozen material (mostly dry ice) evaporates and can no longer hold itself together.

- Explain that comets lose material every time they near the sun, becoming smaller with each pass around the sun. This may eventually destroy the comet. Also, comets have been pulled into the sun. Comet Biela (1846) broke into two pieces as it rounded the sun, with one piece following the other along the orbit, creating twin comets. The two moved further apart when they returned in 1852 and have never been seen since.

- For Internet use, see activity sheets Comets on the Net, Part 1 and Part 2.

Let's Make a Comet

Ingredients	Represent
2 cups (480 mL) water	hydrogen and oxygen gas
10 pounds (4.5 kg) dry ice	carbon dioxide gas
few drops of ammonia	ammonia gas
two or three spoonfuls of sand	solid minerals in the core

Additional Materials: large bowl, large clear plastic bag, gloves, hammer

Instructions

1. Wear gloves when handling the dry ice. Wrap the ice in layers of newspaper and use the hammer to crush it into golf-ball sized chunks.

2. Put the plastic bag into the bowl and dump the ice into it.

3. Add the ammonia and water and press the material into a loose ball.

4. Put in the sand and mix it in the frozen gases to complete your comet.

5. Overlap the bag around the edges of the bowl, leaving the comet exposed.

6. Blow on the comet to simulate the solar wind.

As the air in the classroom (*sun*) heats the frozen gases, they become a vapor. The breath (*solar wind*) blows on the comet, forming a tail which is blown in the opposite direction. A comet's tail spreads out for a million miles in space. This is what we see of the comet in the sky. The core is hidden inside the vapor (*coma*) of the melting gases, just as the core of this comet model is. The tail can be seen for days as the comet makes its way around the sun. Its form increases in size as the comet nears the sun. The tail is longest when the comet reaches the sun, and then the tail shrinks after the comet whips around the sun and returns along its orbit.

Listen to the comet as it melts. It hisses and crackles as the gas pushes its way through holes in the evaporating ice. If you could ride on a comet, you would see jets of gas coming out of it. This action can spin the comet. As the core begins to melt, some dirt or dust loosens and falls away, forming part of the tail. This material is deposited along the comet's orbit, and some is left in Earth's orbit as the comet passes through it. Each time Earth moves through that part of its orbit, gravity pulls some of the material towards our planet. The particles are then called *meteors*, which burn up in the atmosphere. They look like shooting stars. If the meteor survives to hit the ground it is called a *meteorite*.

Comets on the Net, Part 1

Background

No one had ever seen a comet strike a planet until July 1994. A comet headed for Jupiter was discovered by astrogeologists Eugene Shoemaker, his wife Carolyn, and comet hunter David Levy. Visit the Web site of Comet Shoemaker-Levy 9, named after its discoverers to learn more about this fantastic event.

Comet Shoemaker-Levy 9

http://www.jpl.nasa.gov/sl9/

As the comet got near Jupiter, the tremendous gravity of the planet pulled the comet into pieces. These pieces continued to travel toward Jupiter in a chain.

- Look at four images of the chain of comets plunging into Jupiter between July 16 and 22, 1994, at this site.

- Click on the image to see the comet fragments stretched out like a freight train, about to plunge into the planet.

- Click on Back to return to the previous Web page

Remember how fast giant Jupiter rotates (about once every 10 hours), pulling its atmosphere around with it. This can be clearly seen by the way the impact holes in the clouds change.

- Click on *Fragment A Impact* to see a series of pictures showing the impact of this fragment.

- Click on *Hubble Image* to see the impact of the first fragment entering Jupiter's atmosphere.

- Go back and click on *Hubble Images* (July 22, 1994) to see a series of images of the impact site on Jupiter made by Fragment A. Notice how the rapidly moving clouds begin to close into the area and distort the once clear "hole" made by the fragment.

- Click on *Palomar Image of Fragment A-V Impacts* (July 23, 1994). The image shows Jupiter as it would appear to an observer located below the south pole. The individual images were taken over a period of six hours, during which time Jupiter's rapid rotation permitted all nine visible impact sites to be observed. Click on the image to see it enlarged and the fragments identified. The south pole of Jupiter is in the center of the image.

  What would happen if this event were to happen on our planet? Scientists have found evidence that leads them to believe it did happen on Earth about 360 million years ago, while the planet was still in its early stages of development. Look at the radar images of Earth taken from the Space Shuttle in April and October of 1994 at the following Web site to find out about this discovery.

- *Click on Chain of Impact Craters Suggested by Spaceborne Radar Images* (NASA—March 20, 1996) to read the details of this discovery.

Comets on the Net, Part 2

Background

People were terrified of comets since they did not behave like anything else seen in the sky. Unlike the phases of the moon or the motion of the planets, comets appeared without warning and never followed regular paths across the sky. Just like the aurora, stories were invented to explain what comets were.

Edmund Halley (1656-1742) was the first scientist to discover that comets orbited the sun. Using the new laws of motion developed by Isaac Newton, Halley predicted that a comet seen in 1531, 1607, and 1682 (during his lifetime) would return in 1758. Unfortunately, he was no longer alive at that time, but when the comet returned it was named after him. It is the most famous of comets.

Find out about Comet Halley at this Web site and then answer the questions below.

http://seds.lpl.arizona.edu/nineplanets/nineplanets/halley.html

Keyword: Comet Halley

1. What is the average period of Halley's orbit? _____ years

2. Since the comet's last trip was in 1985-86, when should it appear again? _____

3. What were some of the other years the comet was seen? _____ _____ _____ _____ _____

4. Describe Comet Halley's orbit. _____

    _____

5. When the comet came near Earth in 1986, what did scientists do to learn more about it?

6. Describe Comet Halley's nucleus._____

    _____

There are many more comets other than Halley. Visit the following Web site to learn about some of these. Click on the pictures to enlarge them.

    http://planetscapes.com/solar/eng/comet.htm

Read the "Comet Introduction," and then select one of the comets to draw and describe below.

Comet _____

_____

_____

View of a Comet from Earth

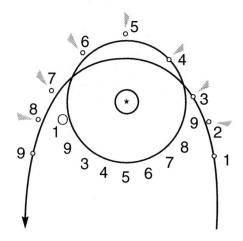

Activity: viewing a comet from Earth

Materials: transparency of View of a Comet from Earth (page 50), awl, round-headed metal snap fastener, clear tape, overhead projector, wet-erase pens for transparencies, drawing paper

- Follow the instructions to assemble the transparencies of the orbits of Earth and a comet. It should look like the drawing (right) when fully assembled.

- Place this on an overhead projector and have students look at the comet in the various locations of its orbit around the sun. Discuss what they see happening to the comet from positions 1-9. (*The tail forms and lengthens as it nears the sun, and then diminishes as it moves away from the sun. The tail always points away from the sun.*)

- Rotate Earth's orbit disk until the planet is at the #1 position. Draw a line with a wet-erase pen from Earth to the comet in the #1 position and another from Earth to the sun. Have students tell what the comet would look like from Earth at this time. (*There is no tail; since the comet is far from the Earth, it would appear very dim and small.*) Ask them where it would appear in the sky relative to the sun. (*It would be about 45° from the sun.*) Erase the lines.

- Move Earth to #2 and draw the lines again. Distribute drawing paper to students and have them draw what the comet would look like from Earth, showing the comet and the sun. (*The comet would have a short tail, difficult to see since Earth's view would be nearly straight at the coma. The comet would be somewhat closer to the sun.*)

- Move Earth to #3 and have the students add the new picture of the comet to their drawing. (*The comet's tail will be longer, and it will be closer to the sun.*)

- Continue moving Earth to each position and have students make drawings to show what they would see. (*The comet would disappear in the glare of the sun at #5.*)

- Add the dates to the comet positions on the transparency and have the students place them on their drawings as well, beginning at #2.

   (1) May 15, (2) July 1, (3) August 1, (4) August 25, (5) September 1, (6) September 8,

   (7) October 2, (8) November 1, (9) December 18

- Ask students to look at the comet's motion and explain it. (*The comet moves slowly from #1 to #3, speeds up between #4 and #6, and then slows down again. As the comet is pulled toward the sun, it slowly adds speed and then moves fastest when close to the sun, slowing down again, once it begins to travel away from the sun.*)

- Place an X on one of the places where the comet crosses through Earth's orbit. Explain that a comet's orbit is usually not in the same plane as Earth's orbit but may come in at an angle so that it actually crosses the orbit at only one point. Ask students what happens to the comet as its core heats up when it gets close to the sun. (*It loses dirt from its core.*)

- Explain that this dirt becomes trapped in Earth's orbit here. Rotate Earth to that spot and ask what happens when Earth returns to this part of its orbit again. (*Earth's gravity pulls some pieces into its atmosphere. We see these as meteors.*)

- *The Visual Dictionary of the Universe* (page 56) and *The Young Astronomer* (page 39) have lists of some of the famous comets and their periods (length of time for one trip around the sun). Show the students that some of these will be visible in their lifetime; however, remind them that there will also be new comets appearing as well.

View of a Comet from Earth *(cont.)*

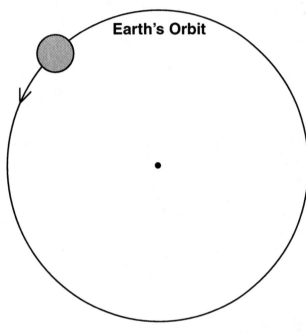

Earth's Orbit

Assembly Instructions

1. Cut along the dotted line below.

2. Cut around Earth's orbit, being sure to leave the Earth and orbit outline.

3. Superimpose the dots in the centers of the sun and Earth's orbit. Use tape to hold the two images together in this position.

4. Place the transparencies over the hole of a tape dispenser, so the dots are in the center of the hole.

5. Push the awl through the dots to make a hole large enough to insert the snap. Be sure there is enough clearance so that Earth's circle can be turned freely around the sun.

Cut along this dotted line.

- -

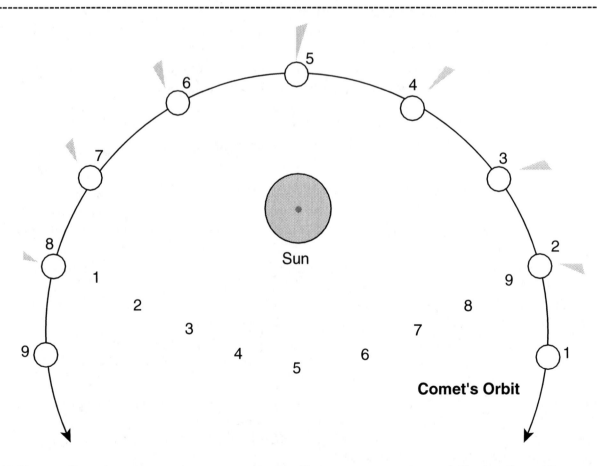

Sun

Comet's Orbit

Meteors

Meteor Showers (*Guide to Space*, page 64; *The Visual Dictionary of the Universe*, page 48) A list of annual meteor showers can be found in Guide to Space, and pictures of meteors and a meteor shower are shown in *The Visual Dictionary of the Universe.*

Background

Meteoroids are the smallest particles orbiting the sun, most no larger than grains of sand. After studying the evolution of meteor streams, astronomers think the clouds of meteoroids orbiting the sun were produced by comets. Because of their small size, meteoroids cannot be observed moving through space. However, satellites recovered by manned spacecraft have shown pits in their skin, caused by the impact of meteoroids.

When meteoroids enter Earth's atmosphere, they are then referred to as *meteors*. They become visible as a result of friction caused by air molecules rubbing against the particles speeding through the atmosphere. The friction causes them to glow blue or white, but other colors have been reported. Most meteors completely burn up at altitudes between 60 and 80 miles (96-128 km) and are rarely seen for more than a few seconds. About 100 tons of meteor dust falls on Earth daily.

Occasionally, a large meteor will not burn up completely as it moves through Earth's atmosphere. The subsequent pieces that fall to Earth's surface are known as *meteorites*.

Activity: learning about meteor showers

Materials: access to the Internet

- Review how comets crossing Earth's orbit leave debris in that area. When Earth passes through that part of its orbit, some debris is pulled in it by Earth's gravity. Explain that not all the material is pulled in at one time, so we can predict that when Earth reaches these points on its orbit, there will be a meteor shower. The number of meteors pulled into the atmosphere depends upon how many are within Earth's gravitational pull. Share the background information about the size of meteors and the differences between meteoroids, meteors, and meteorites.

- Show the list of meteor showers from the *Guide to Space*. Students will find that they occur every month. Some of these showers are more dramatic than others.

- Have students visit these Web sites for information about two of the best meter showers.

Perseid Shower (August)**:**
http://comets.amsmeteors.org/meteors/showers/perseids.html

Leonid Meteor Shower (November):

For the history of this shower and how it helped scientists make the connection between meteor showers and comets, go to: http://comets.amsmeteors.org/meteors/showers/leonidhis.htmI

To see spectacular photographs of the Leonid meteor shower, go to:

http://comets.amsmeteors.org/meteors/showers/leonidphotos.html

When an extra bright meteor burns up on its way through the atmosphere, it is called a fireball.

Visit the following Web sites to learn more information about two exciting fireballs.

Fireball of February 26, 1996
http://seds.lpl.arizona.edu/nineplanets/nineplanets/pxmisc.html#Comets

Scan down to *Meteorites* and then click on *caption* following "a fireball captured on video." Look at the picture and read about this recent fireball.

Meteors (cont.)

Activity: learning about impact craters on Earth

Materials: Internet access

- Explain that some meteorites, and possibly even comets, have struck Earth in the past. Many scientists believe that a large object, perhaps a comet, struck Earth 65 million years ago near the Yucatan Peninsula area of Mexico. Debris from this impact was thrown into the atmosphere so high that it took many years before it settled back to Earth. This caused climatic changes leading to the death of many animals, including the dinosaurs. When astrogeologist Eugene Shoemaker studied the .75 mile (1.2 km) wide Barringer Crater in Arizona, he found evidence that it was not an old volcano, as many thought, but resulted from an 11,000-ton iron meteorite plowing into Earth 49,000 years ago. See information about this meteor crater in *The Visual Dictionary of the Universe*, page 39.

- To learn more about meteors and meteorites, have the students visit the following Web site. There are excellent pictures of various types of meteorites, including one that some scientists believe came from Mars. It was discovered in Antarctica.

Meteors and Meteorites

http://seds.lpl.arizona.edu/nineplanets/nineplanets/meteorites.html

http://www.skypub.com/sights/meteors/meteors.shtml

http://www.solarviews.com/solar/eng/meteor.htm

Keyword: Meteors and Meteorites

Activity: simulating impact craters

Materials: three aluminum roasting pans, flour, three spheres of the same size but different masses—e.g., a glass marble, a metal ball bearing, a Styrofoam ball

- Fill the aluminum pans with flour.
- Divide the students into three groups and assign each to a different pan. Give each group one of the spheres. Have one member of each group stand so that he or she can drop the sphere from a height of six feet. As the sphere is dropped, the other members of the group should watch what the impact looks like so they can describe it.

- Let each groups drop their spheres into the flour from the same height.
- Ask them the following questions:

Which sphere created the largest crater? (*The one with the greatest mass.*)

Why are the craters different sizes? (*The spheres are all different masses.*)

If each sphere were a meteorite falling on the earth's surface, which would do the most danger? (*The sphere with the greatest mass.*)

Asteroids

Minor Planets (*Guide to Space*, page 39)

In the *Guide to Space*, show students the picture of Ida, an asteroid 32 miles (51 km) long that has its own moon, Dactyl.

Background

Asteroids, or minor planets, have been described as "mountains in space." They are large rocks typically ranging from a few feet to several hundred miles across. Most asteroids move between the orbits of Mars and Jupiter in what is often called the "asteroid belt." They appear star-like in telescopes. Against the background of stars, their motion is usually so slow that several hours may pass before any movement is noticed. Most asteroids within the asteroid belt never come closer than 100 million miles from Earth, but there are some which come closer to—and even cross—Earth's orbit. These objects can occasionally pass within a few million miles of us, or even within the orbit of the moon. They move so fast in this location that the change is apparent after only a few minutes. Asteroids within the asteroid belt can be observed every year, while ones passing especially close to Earth may be visible for only a few weeks or months.

Astronomers distinguish asteroids and comets on the basis of their telescopic appearance. If the object is star-like in appearance, it is called an *asteroid*. If it has a visible atmosphere or tail, it is a comet. Scientists do not distinguish between asteroids and comets in methods to warn of impacting Earth. Both can collide with our planet.

Earth is located in a swarm of comets and asteroids that can, and do, collide with it periodically. The solar system has a huge population of asteroids and comets, remnants of its origin. From time to time some are bumped into orbits that cross the orbits of Earth and other planets. Spacecraft exploration of terrestrial (solid) planets and most of the moons of planets shows cratered surfaces made by continuous impacts from projectiles.

Additional evidence about asteroids near Earth has been collected since the first asteroid was discovered nearly 60 years ago. Improvements in telescopic search techniques have resulted in the discovery of dozens of near-Earth asteroids and short-period comets each year. The role of impacts in Earth's geological history, its ecosphere, and the evolution of life itself, has become a major topic of discussion among scientists.

The possible dangers of such impacts focused when, in 1989, father-and-son geologists team, Luis and Walter Alvarez, found evidence indicating that an asteroid estimated at 6-10 miles (10-16 km) long impacted Earth 65 million years ago, resulting in extinction of many life forms and ending the age of dinosaurs. The greatest risk is from the impact of the largest objects—those with diameters greater than 1/2 mile (1 km). Such impacts may occur once to several times per million years and would affect the entire planet.

Activity: learning about dangers of asteroids on Earth

Materials: Internet access, transparencies of Impact Craters on Earth, Near Earth Asteroids (pages 56 and 57)

- Share the background information on asteroids. Recently, scientists have been able to alert the public and congress to the possibility of an asteroid or comet colliding with Earth. The NASA Spaceguard Survey, serving as an early warning system, is dedicated to identifying those near Earth asteroids potentially dangerous to Earth.

- Show and discuss the transparencies of impact crater sites and near-Earth asteroids.

Asteroids *(cont.)*

- Have students visit this Web site to see examples of an asteroid which came near crashing into Earth, and one which exploded so close it created much damage.

NASA Safeguard Survey
http://impact.arc.nasa.gov/reports/spaceguard/sg_2.html

To the Teacher: There is lengthy information at this site to read later. Scan down to Figure 2:2 and read and discuss the information about the two asteroids. Click on the pictures to enlarge them. If possible, use one monitor to show the images to the entire class. Share the information below as you show and discuss the pictures.

Figure 2:2 On August 10, 1972, an alert photographer in Grand Teton National Park recorded the passage of an object estimated at 11 yards (10 m) in diameter and weighing several thousand tons. The object traveled over 922 miles (1,475 km) at about nine miles (15 km) per second. It burned for 101 seconds crossing through the atmosphere, although most meteors burn only one to two seconds. It came within 60 miles (96 km) of Earth's surface before skipping out of the atmosphere like a rock across water.

On June 30, 1908, at 7:40 A.M., a cosmic projectile exploded perhaps five miles (8 km) above ground over Siberia, Russia. Scientists think it may have been a comet or a piece of a comet at least 200 feet (60 m) long. It flattened 1250 sq. miles (2,000 sq. km) of forest in the Tunguska region. The energy released was about 12 megatons as estimated from airwaves recorded on meteorological barographs in England, or perhaps 20 megatons as estimated from the radius of destruction. Evidence suggests fires were ignited up to nine miles (15 km) from the outer edges of the blast. If a similar event were to occur in a populated area today, hundreds of thousands of people would die, buildings would be flattened over an area 12.5 miles (20 km) in radius, and damage would be in hundreds of billions of dollars.

Activity: learning about the Torino Scale

Materials: transparency of Frequency and Magnitudes of Cosmic Impacts (page 58)

- Show the transparency of page 58, depicting the estimated frequency of asteroid impacts compared to the magnitude of their energy. This data shows the pattern for the majority of events and is based on the present population of comets and asteroids and evidence from lunar craters. Discuss the graph and add the new data. You will notice that the Tunguska event follows the pattern, but the Arizona asteroid does not.

- Explain that NASA launched the *Deep Space 1* unmanned spacecraft in October 1998. On July 29 it flew by asteroid Braille, getting low-resolution black-and-white photos that gave scientists clues about its composition and geologic history. Have students visit the following Web site to learn more about this mission and others in NASA's programs.

Deep Space 1—flyby of asteroid
http://www.jpl.nasa.gov/ds1news/

- This Web site is constantly updated. Scan to pictures and click on *Artists Conceptions*. Click on *caption* to read the information about the picture and then return to click on the picture to see it enlarged. Return to the Home Page and click on "Asteroid Mystery in Space," showing how scientists are using the new data to see if the Braille asteroid was once a part of Vesta, a large asteroid discovered in 1807.

Asteroids *(cont.)*

- The Torino Scale was recently created by Dr. Richard P. Binzel at the Department of Earth, Atmospheric, and Planetary Sciences, at the Massachusetts Institute of Technology (MIT). This 0-10 range scale rates the asteroids' potential for creating damage, much as scales today rate hurricanes. Identification of where these asteroids are, relative to Earth, and their rank on the scale will provide an early-warning system. If the asteroid is far enough away, measures may be taken to deflect or destroy it.

- Have students visit the following Web site to learn about the Torino Scale.

   Asteroid Impacts Hazards: Torino Scale
   http://impact.arc.nasa.gov/torino/index.html

- Divide the students into groups and have them select question(s) from the Web site list (below) to answer.

   1. What is the Torino Scale used for?

   2. Why is the Torino Scale needed?

   3. How does the Torino Scale work? (Print out a copy of the Torino Scale in color if possible.

   4. How does an object get its Torino Scale number? (Gather information from the following Web site.)

   Graph of Torino Scale for Asteroids and Comets
   http://impact.arc.nasa.gov/torino/prof.html

   5. Can the Torino Scale value for an object change?

   6. How did the Torino Scale get its name? (This group should locate Torino, Italy, on a map.)

- Check the information provided for each question before assigning them since some questions will be briefly answered while others are quite lengthy. Thus, the shorter ones may be combined.

Activity: finding current information about asteroids

Materials: science magazines and newspapers, news broadcasts, NASA Web site

- The topic of the danger from near Earth asteroids has changed from pure speculation to scientific study. It is now a topic which frequently appears in the news. Have students collect asteroid information from periodicals, news broadcasts or at Web sites such as the NASA one on *Deep Space 1* that is constantly updated. Encourage all students to participate by providing time each day for students to share news items they may have brought in or heard on broadcasts. Dedicate bulletin board space for the news articles and summaries of TV or radio reports to be posted for all to see. Be sure to include the names of the students on their items.

- Have the students create a survey to collect information on public knowledge of asteroids and the potential threat they pose. They should compose a brief summary of what they have learned from the interview that can be given to people they surveyed. Graph and analyze the survey results.

- Consider having students write articles describing what they have learned from this study and submit these to the school or local newspaper.

Impact Craters on Earth

(as of December 1991)

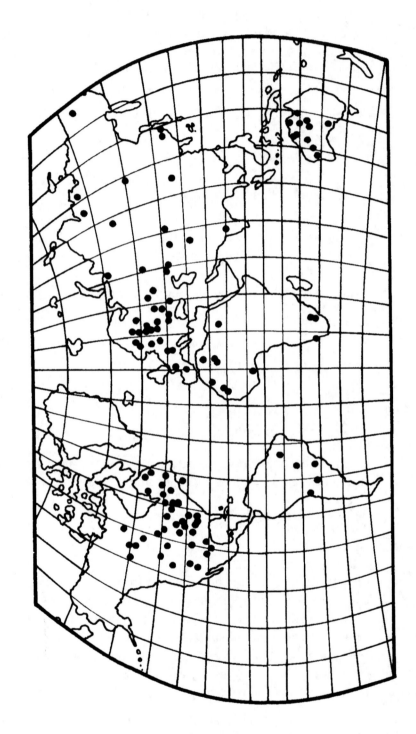

Approximately 130 land impact craters have been identified. They range from 224 to 320 miles (140 to 200) km in diameter and from recent to about two billion years in age. Notice that most craters have been identified in Australia, North America, and Eastern Europe. This is partly because the surface areas here have been relatively stable for considerable geologic periods (thus preserving the early geologic record) and because active search programs have been conducted in these areas. More impact craters are being discovered now that there is the capability of seeing them from Earth-orbiting satellites and the Space Shuttle. Impact craters on the floor of the ocean are not included in this graphic but do exist. These are more difficult to find, and many would have eroded beyond recognition since the time of their creation.

Art courtesy of R. A. F. Grieve, Geological Survey of Canada

http://impact.arc.nasa.gov/reports/spaceguard/sg_1.html

Orbits of Near-Earth Asteroids

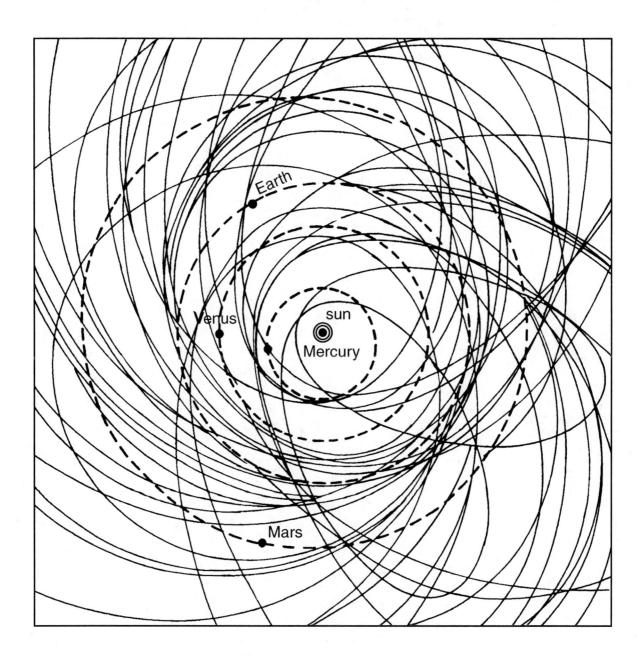

The inner planets' orbits are shown as dotted ellipses around the sun. The solid orbits superimposed on them are the 100 largest known near-Earth asteroids. This drawing makes it appear that constant collisions should be occurring between the asteroids and Earth. Of course, we know these collisions are rare. The reasons for this are listed below.

1. While the four planets' orbits are on the same plane, the asteroids' orbits are at various angles to the plane. This is similar to several airplanes flying stacked up over an airport.

2. Earth and the asteroids are seldom in the same location in their respective orbits when those orbits overlap. Therefore, the asteroids are too far from Earth to be pulled in by its gravity. Even though it seldom happens, there is the possibility of a change in one of these asteroid orbits or the appearance of an uncharted one, which could result in impact with Earth in the future.

Frequency and Magnitudes of Cosmic Impacts

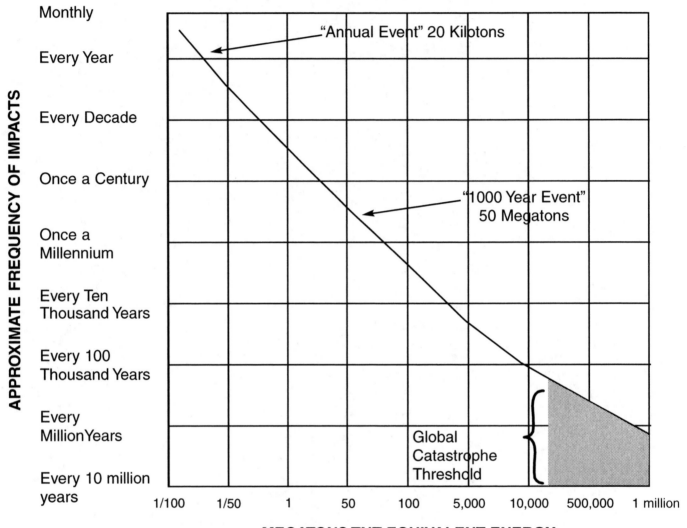

1 kiloton = the explosive force of 1,000 tons of TNT

1 megaton = explosive force of 1,000,000 tons of TNT

Which are more likely to happen—small or large impacts?

Add the following events to this graph:

- The 1908 cosmic projectile which exploded over Tunguska, Russia, was about 12 megatons.

- The meteor which crashed into Arizona about 50,000 years ago was 10–20 megatons.

The asteroid which plowed into the Yucatan Peninsula of Mexico 65 million years ago was estimated to be 1 billion megatons.

Note: The chance of Earth being hit by something large enough to destroy crops worldwide within your lifetime is about 1 in 10,000.

Sky Pictures

Constellations: (*The Young Astronomer*, pages 25-30); (*The Visual Dictionary of the Universe*, pages 15-17)

Several activities in *The Young Astronomer* help students study the night sky. These include making a quadrant or simple sextant to determine latitude (page 27) and a device to show the positions of the sun, Earth, and zodiac constellations (pages 28 and 29). There is also an activity for creating a model of the constellation Cygnus (the Swan or Northern Cross) on page 30. Both books have excellent constellation maps.

Background

Constellations (pages 61 and 62) are images of human and animal figures in the sky, using stars like dot-to-dot pictures. Most of these were designed over 2,000 years ago, spread symmetrically around a point above Earth's North Pole. Today Polaris (the North Star) is over the Pole, but that was not so then. As Earth rotates on its axis, it wobbles like a top so that the north axis pole moves in a circular motion over a 26,000-year period. This changes the locations of constellations.

The 12 zodiac constellations are located along the *ecliptic*, the path the sun appears to follow as Earth revolves around it. The moon and planets also follow this path and are seen against the band of zodiac constellations. Astronomy had its beginnings in astrology, a belief that human behavior was controlled by the motion of the planets, sun, and moon within zodiac constellations. We know now that there is no connection between how these celestial bodies move and what happens to anyone on Earth. But astrologers carefully recorded the changing locations of these bodies, and this valuable data later helped astronomers understand more about the motions of planets.

The sun's position within zodiac constellations is different today. Along with the wobble of Earth, the planet does not return to exactly the same location in its orbit at the same time each year. Thus, the sun gradually moves into the next zodiac constellation. The months when the sun is in each zodiac constellation (pages 61 and 62) do not match the dates in horoscopes, but are astronomically correct for the present time.

The zodiac and other constellations serve as useful maps of the sky, helping us locate planets, comets, and other celestial bodies. Monthly constellation charts can help students locate patterns in the sky and find the planets moving among these star patterns.

Activity: simulating the sun's path through the zodiac constellations

Materials: zodiac constellations (pages 61 and 62), overhead projector, 12 sheets of large black construction paper, chalk or white marker, clamp-on light with 150-watt bulb

Lesson Preparation

- Make transparencies of the zodiac constellations. Project them onto the large black paper individually; use the white marker to trace the stars (dots) and lines. The sizes of the dots denote brightness, not size. The larger dots are brighter stars.

- Include the constellation name, when the sun is there, and when it is seen.

- Use a large room for this lesson. Using a string four feet (122 cm) long with a loop at one end and a piece of chalk tied to the other, make a circle in the center of the floor. Have someone hold the loop of the string in the center of the floor, stretch out the string, and use the chalk to draw the circle. Shorten the string to 2.5 feet (76 cm) and draw another circle within the first, using the same center point. Place the lamp in the center of these circles at the students' eye level.

Sky Pictures *(cont.)*

Procedure

- Share the background information about the zodiac constellations, using the transparencies to enable students to see what they look like.

- Take the students to a large room. Have 12 students hold the zodiac pictures. Have them spread out equally around the large circle. The constellations should be in order of the numbers, moving in a clockwise direction around the circle.

- Have the remaining students stand around the inner circle, facing the constellations. Turn on the bright light and turn off the room lights. Tell students that the bright light is the sun and they are the Earth. Have them spin slowly in their positions in a counterclockwise direction (west to east) to simulate day and night. Day is when they face the sun (light), night when they face away from the light and see the stars.

- Explain that if they could go north out beyond the solar system, they would see the Earth move around the sun in a counterclockwise direction. Let them begin to walk slowly in a counterclockwise direction around the circle, looking at the constellations as they do so. Point out that these change as they move. Explain that from Earth we see new constellations gradually appearing in the eastern sky, as those in the west gradually disappear below the western horizon. It takes 12 months to get back to the original set of constellations. Have them walk all the way around the circle, mentally marking the constellation they see at the beginning, and stopping there after walking around the circle. Explain that they have just gone through one year.

- Have students collect on one side of the light, face towards it, and try to see the constellations opposite it. Explain that the sun is so bright we can't see the stars beyond it. Tell the students that the 12 zodiac constellations correspond to the location of the sun during each of the 12 months. When the sun is "in" one of them (e.g., Leo), we can't see the constellation. Only when we go into space, where sunlight is not scattered by Earth's atmosphere, can we see the stars and sun together. Even then, some of the stars near the sun are hard to see due to its bright light. We can catch glimpses of bright stars and planets during a total solar eclipse, when we can see beyond our atmosphere.

- Explain that planets and our moon move around the sun on a plane, like a huge dinner plate with the sun in the center. The zodiac constellations lie beyond this plane, appearing roughly east to west across Earth's sky. The planets, moon, and sun never appear in the sky north or south of this band of stars.

- Review the zodiac constellations and look closely at the figures these star patterns are supposed to represent. Ask students which ones most resemble the pictures. These are Leo, (lion), Scorpio (scorpion), and Taurus (bull—face and horns only).

- Make enlarged copies of some of these constellations without the lines for the students to make their own constellations. Have them use the patterns of the stars (dots) to turn them into pictures of things familiar to them.

- Have students research the legends connected with constellations. Have them use the Internet and various reference materials.

Zodiac Constellations

To the Student: The 12 constellations in these pictures are those which appear along the path the sun seems to follow in the sky as the Earth moves around it. Long ago, people thought that our lives were controlled by the location of planets in these constellations. Today, we know that the planets move in orbit around the sun and have no influence on humans at all. The shapes of the constellations form a useful map in the sky which helps us locate planets which are seen against these stars. A planet looks like an extra star in the constellation, but it gradually moves into the next constellation.

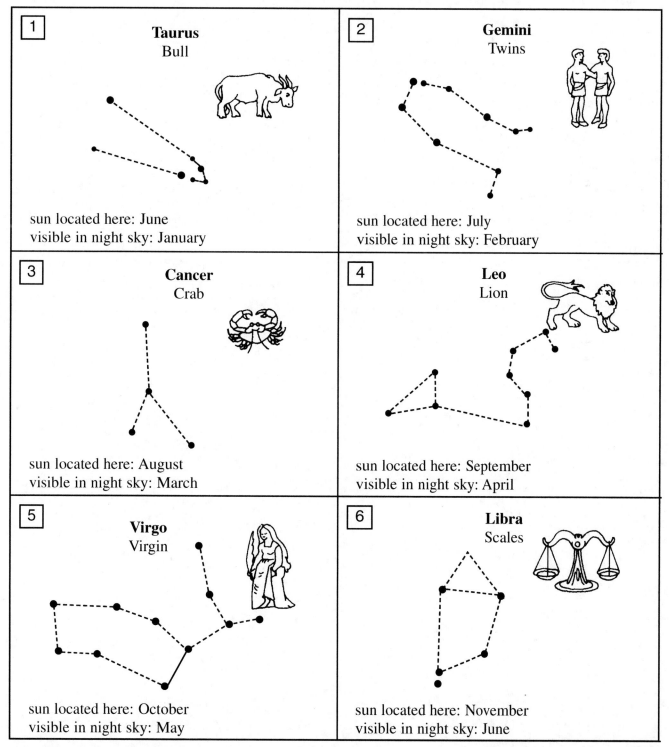

1 **Taurus** Bull sun located here: June visible in night sky: January	**2** **Gemini** Twins sun located here: July visible in night sky: February
3 **Cancer** Crab sun located here: August visible in night sky: March	**4** **Leo** Lion sun located here: September visible in night sky: April
5 **Virgo** Virgin sun located here: October visible in night sky: May	**6** **Libra** Scales sun located here: November visible in night sky: June

Zodiac Constellations *(cont.)*

The month stated for viewing each constellation is the best month to see it. However, it will also be visible the month before and after. Visibility of these constellations also depends on the latitude of your location.

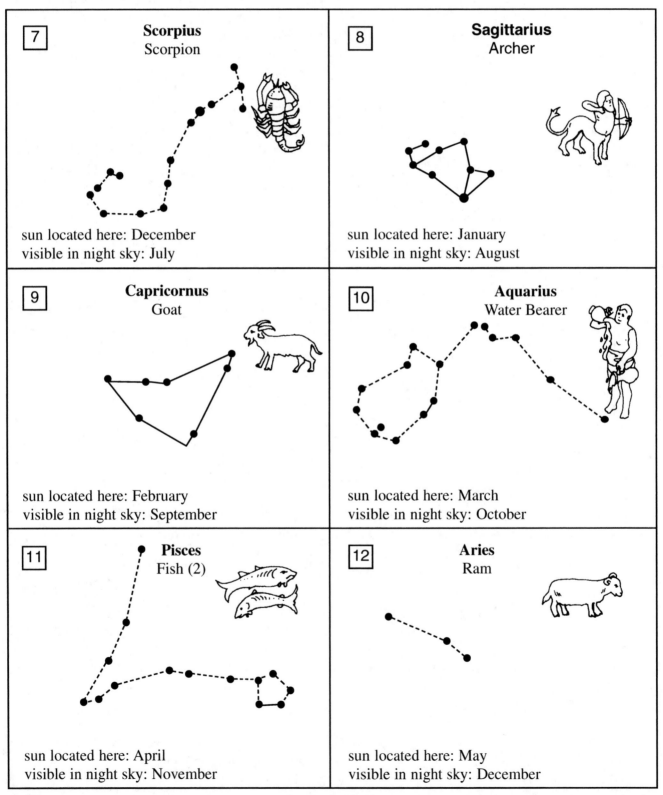

7   **Scorpius**
Scorpion

sun located here: December
visible in night sky: July

8   **Sagittarius**
Archer

sun located here: January
visible in night sky: August

9   **Capricornus**
Goat

sun located here: February
visible in night sky: September

10   **Aquarius**
Water Bearer

sun located here: March
visible in night sky: October

11   **Pisces**
Fish (2)

sun located here: April
visible in night sky: November

12   **Aries**
Ram

sun located here: May
visible in night sky: December

Ursa Major

Activity: viewing the North Polar Constellations

Materials: transparency and copies of North Circumpolar Constellations chart (page 64)

If possible, copy this chart on tagboard.

- Show the transparency of the chart and explain how it should be used in the sky. Give each student a copy to rotate so that the present month is on top.

- Tell the students to take the chart home and use it this evening to match the stars to those they see in the sky. Explain that Polaris will appear at an angle above the northern horizon equal to the latitude of the location from which it is being viewed.

- At the next class, have students tell what they could see. Encourage them to continue using the chart until they are able to make out all those constellations.

Activity: using Ursa Major to locate other constellations

Materials: transparency and copies of The Big Dipper's Magic Arrows (page 65)

- Show the transparency of North Circumpolar Constellations and discuss the shape and location of Ursa Major. Note its shape as the Big Dipper. Show how the two stars in the bowl point to the North Star (Polaris) and are thus called "pointer stars."

- Let the students see the transparency of the Big Dipper's Magic Arrows. Follow instructions to see how the Big Dipper is used to locate nearby constellations.

- Provide students with copies of this chart to take home to use tonight.

- Arrange a meeting at night on the school playground or another dark location. Students and their families may gather to learn how to identify the North Circumpolar Constellations and use the Big Dipper to find other constellations. This is best done in winter, when dark comes early and skies are usually clearer.

Activity: making a model of Ursa Major

Materials: copies and transparency of Making a Model of the Big Dipper (page 66) and transparency of Changes in the Dipper (page 67), enlarged picture of the dipper today (page 67)

- Cut away one end of the shoeboxes and lids; spray the insides of these with black paint.

- Enlarge the image of how the dipper looks today so it will fit in one end of the shoebox; make copies for each shoebox. Use a transparency of this enlargement to show that the Big Dipper is made up of seven bright stars, each of which has been named.

- Although from Earth we see these stars in the pattern of a dipper, they are not all the same distance from us. Tell students that distances are so great in space that astronomers measure them in light years. A light year is the distance light can travel in a year. Since light travels at 186,322 miles per second, a light year is about 6 trillion miles.

- Use the transparency of page 66 to explain the template for a model of the Big Dipper. Explain that the distance of each star is represented by its distance on this template from Earth (E). The length of the string for each star represents its position as seen from Earth.

- Divide students into groups and provide the materials on the template.

- When the students finish, use the transparency of Changes in the Dipper to explain how this constellation has changed and will continue to do so in the future. Discuss how the stars Alkais and Dubhe move during 100,000 years. Tell the students that all the constellations we see will also evolve into other shapes in the future.

North Circumpolar Constellations

Instructions: Go to a place where you can see the stars. Take a flashlight with you. Cover the light with your fingers when using it to see the chart to cut down on the light so you can also see the sky. Face north and rotate this chart so the present month is at the top. This should match your view of the sky at about 9 p.m. If you are using this before 9 p.m., rotate the chart slightly counterclockwise.

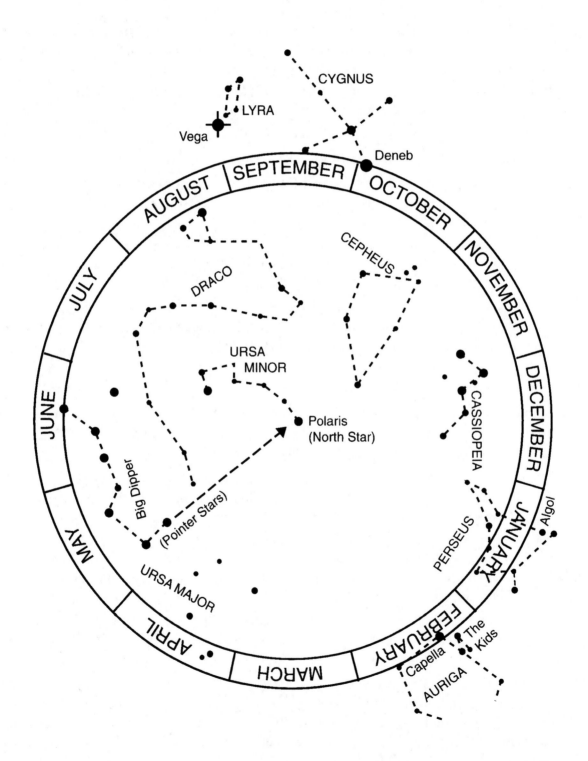

The Big Dipper's Magic Arrows

You can use the Big Dipper to help locate other nearby stars and constellations. The names of constellations on this chart are all written in CAPITAL letters.

Instructions

- Use the pointer stars at the end of the bowl of the Big Dipper to locate the North Star, Polaris. What is the constellation to which Polaris is attached?

- Return to the Big Dipper and pretend to fill the bowl with water. Poke an imaginary hole in the bowl. The water will now drip across the sky and fall on the back of Leo the Lion.

- Trace the arc in the handle of the dipper and "arc to Arcturus." This is a giant red star at the base of Bootes, the kite-shaped constellation. This star is much larger than our sun. If it were in the center of our solar system, it would stretch all the way out to the orbit of Mars.

- Now, slide across the sky from Arcturus to Spica, a bright star in the constellation Virgo.

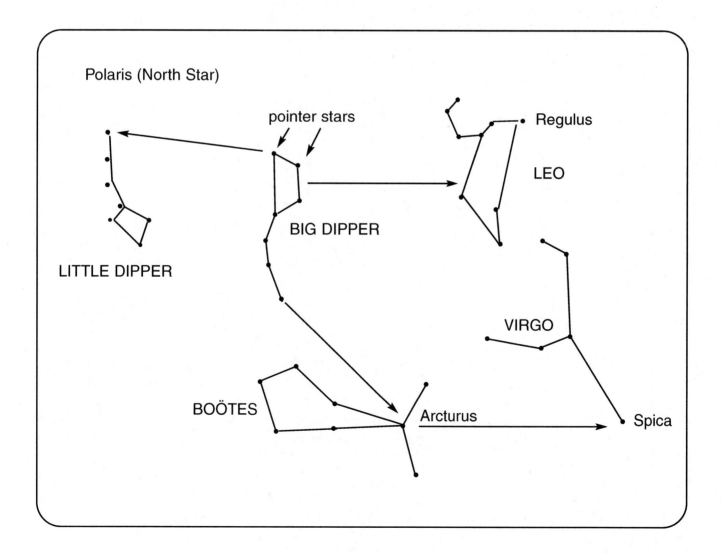

Making a Model of the Big Dipper

Materials: black paint, shoebox, lid, black thread, aluminum foil, scissors, clear tape, picture of the Big Dipper

Instructions

1. Cut seven pieces of thread into six 6-inch (15.2 cm) lengths. Tape them to the dots on this template so that they will hang straight down from the dots.

2. Make seven small balls from the foil and tie each to the end of the string so it is level with the X. Cut away the extra string.

3. Trim this template so it will fit inside the shoebox lid and then tape it in place so the E will be at the cutaway end.

4. Glue today's Big Dipper picture (page 67) inside the shoebox opposite the opening.

5. Put the box on a table and look directly into it from about eight inches away. E stands for *Earth*. As you look from Earth, you see the pattern of a dipper, even though the stars are not all the same distance from you. Compare what you see with the picture of the Big Dipper at the back of the box.

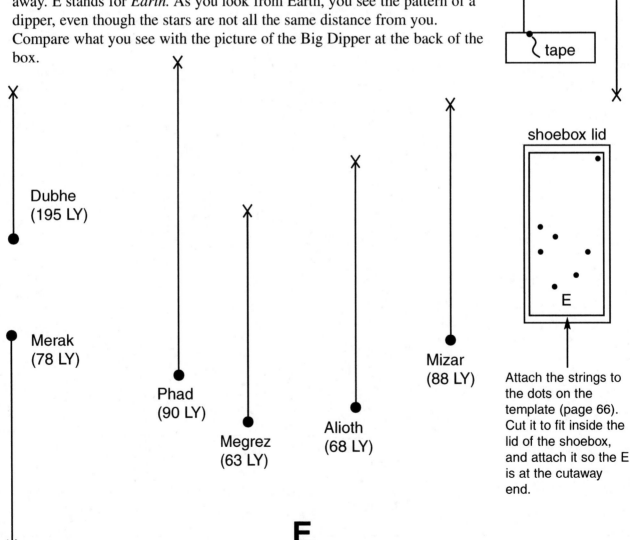

Alkaid
(210 LY)

tape

shoebox lid

Dubhe
(195 LY)

Merak
(78 LY)

Phad
(90 LY)

Megrez
(63 LY)

Alioth
(68 LY)

Mizar
(88 LY)

E

Attach the strings to the dots on the template (page 66). Cut it to fit inside the lid of the shoebox, and attach it so the E is at the cutaway end.

E

Changes in the Dipper

The stars which form the Big Dipper are slowly moving, and thus the shape of this constellation looked different in the past and will continue to change.

50,000 Years Ago

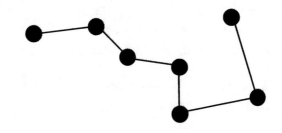

Today

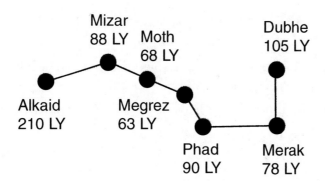

50,000 Years from Now

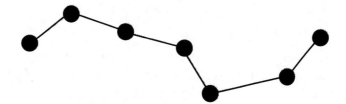

Retrograde Motion of Mars

Activity: plotting the path of Mars through the constellations

Materials: Mars Motion in 1971 and Explaining Retrograde Motion of Mars (pages 69 and 70)

Background

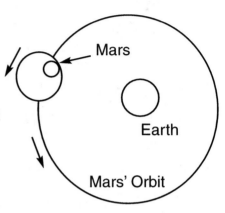

Ancient astronomers (astrologers) mapped the positions of planets moving gradually through zodiac constellations. They saw that planets moved across the sky from east to west each day. However, they also slipped eastward throughout the year. Since astronomers believed the planets were traveling around Earth, they assumed the paths would always move eastward, like the sun. What they observed was very different. The planets did move eastward, but from time to time they would slow down, stop, and then begin moving westward. Gradually, they would slow down again until they stopped and resumed their eastward motion again. Thus, they appeared to be making loops in their paths. The loops varied in size with each planet, and not every planet was looping at the same time. This was finally explained by the theory that the planets were traveling around Earth within their own circular orbits, called *epicycles.*

Later, it was proved that the planets revolve around the sun, not Earth. Now, a different explanation for this backwards, or *retrograde*, motion was needed.

Mars will be used as the example in this activity to show students what the retrograde loop looks like when plotted against the constellations and why we see this happening.

- Make transparencies of Mars Motion in 1971 and Explaining Retrograde Motion. Cut and assemble the latter according to the instructions.

- Show the transparency of Mars Motion in 1971. Read the information about the diagram.

- Have students refer to drawing and chart to answer the following:

  1. (*Trace the path of Mars from #1 to #13.*) Look at the path. What is the direction of Mars from #1 position to #4? (*eastward*)

  2. Describe what happened after that. (*The planet began to move westward after #5 until #9 when it began to move eastward again.*)

  3. Was there any change in Mars' appearance at this time? (*Yes, it increased in size from #1 to its largest size on August 11 at position #7. It then began to become smaller*)

  4. What happened to its brightness? (*Mars became brighter as it grew in size and then dimmer as it reduced in size.*)

  5. Why would Mars change in size and brightness? (*As it gets closer to Earth, it would appear to increase in size and brightness.*)

- Show the students the transparency of Explaining Retrograde Motion of Mars. Point out the orbits of Mars and Earth are not centered on the sun. Show that Mars takes longer than 12 months to make one complete trip around the sun. Place a finger from each hand on the position 1 for both planets. Rotate Earth's orbit, keeping your fingers moving to 2. As you do this for all positions, pause to analyze the distances and direction of Mars. Notice that Mars appears to lag behind Earth (retrograde) from 4 until 10, after which Mars begins to catch up with Earth again.

Have the students find where Mars appears brightest (4 or 5). Dimmest (12).

Mars Motion in 1971

During the summer of 1971, Earth passed closer to Mars than it had since 1924. Not until 2003 will our planet be closer to Mars than it was in August 1971.

CAPRICORNUS

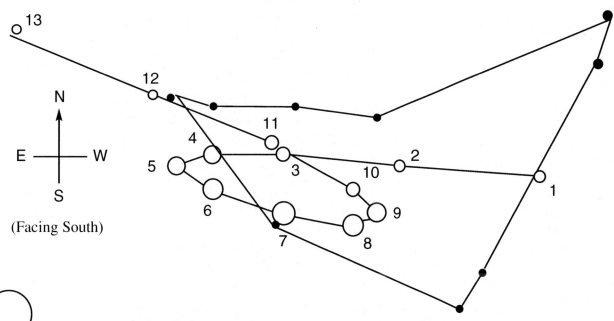

Open circles show the positions of Mars in the constellation Capricornus, beginning May 13, 1971. Stars are solid black circles; their sizes indicate their brightness.

Sizes of the open circles indicate the changing size of Mars as seen through a telescope. Mars also became brighter as it increased in size. The numbers by or in the circles correspond to the dates listed below.

Number	Date	Distance from Earth	Apparent Magnitude (*Brightness)
1	May 13	75 million miles	-0.4
2	May 28	64	-0.7
3	June 12	55	-1.2
4	June 27	47	-1.6
5	July 12	41	2.1
6	July 27	36	-2.4
7	August 11	35	-2.6
8	August 26	36	-2.4
9	September 10	40	-2.1
10	September 25	46	-1.6
11	October 10	54	-1.2
12	October 23	63	-0.6
13	November 9	72	-0.5

*The higher the negative number, the brighter Mars appeared.

Explaining Retrograde Motion of Mars

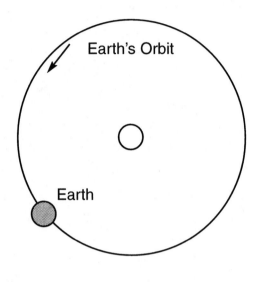

Instructions

1. Make a transparency of this page.

2. Cut along the dotted line.

3. Cut out Earth's orbit, being sure not to cut away the circle or the planet.

4. Superimpose the circle in the center of Earth's orbit over the sun. Use tape to hold the two images in this position.

5. Place the transparencies over the hole of a tape dispenser so the dots are in the center of the hole.

6. Push the awl through the dots to make a hole large enough to insert the snap. Be sure there is enough clearance so that Earth's orbit can be turned freely around the sun.

Cut along this line.

Retrograde Motion of Mars as Seen from Earth

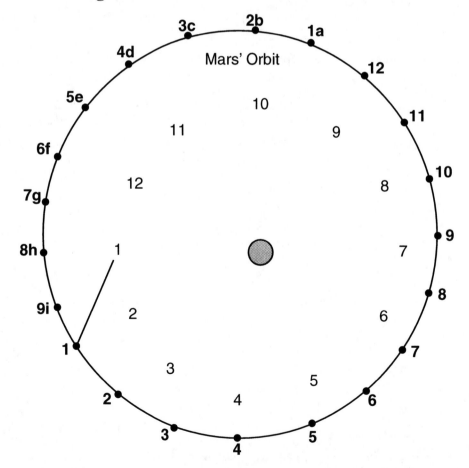

Earth's Journey Through the Universe

Where is Earth located in the universe? (*The Visual Dictionary of the Universe* and *Guide to Space*)
Introduce this series of lessons by sharing the information from *The Visual Dictionary of the Universe*—The Universe (pages 6 and 7), Galaxies (pages 8 and 9), The Milky Way Galaxy (pages 10 and 11), and *Guide to Space*—The Milky Way (pages 44 and 45) and Galaxies (pages 46 and 47)

Activity: simulating the motions of Earth as it travels through the Universe

Materials

- copy of Earth's Journey Cue Cards (page 72) for each student
  bright light source such as a 150-watt bulb in a clamp-on fixture
- globe with two small cardboard people attached
- copies of Earth's Journey Models (page 73)
- calculators (one per student)
- How Fast Are You Traveling? data sheet (page 74) for each student
- *Optional*: The Universe, poster (available through National Geographic Society, Washington, D.C. See Resource section.)

Lesson Preparation

1. Enlarge pictures of Earth's Journey Models beginning with the Solar System as the smallest and the Universe as the largest.
2. Copy Earth's Journey Cue Cards on card stock and cut them apart.
3. Prepare display space for Earth's Journey Through the Universe models.
4. Stick a small cardboard cutout of a person on the globe at your location and another at the equator, on the other side of Earth.
5. In the center of a room, place a light that can be darkened for the first two legs of the journey.

Procedure

- Use pages 48 and 49, "The Universe" from *Guide to Space*, to introduce this activity. (*Note*: The author describes a trip aboard the space shuttle from Earth through the Milky Way and beyond. This is impossible since the shuttle is capable of orbiting Earth but not traveling through space beyond Earth. The author does not tell the speed of travel in this journey, so the length of time given to reach each location is not meaningful.)
- Tell students they are going to do a simulation to help them find Earth's location in the Universe and determine the speeds at which our planet is traveling.
- Distribute Earth's Journey Cue Cards and props to six students. Let them become familiar with their parts; then assemble the class near the light.
- Turn on the light (sun) and turn off the room lights. Have two students demonstrate (1) Earth rotates on its axis and (2) Earth orbits the sun at 66,660 mph (106,656 km).
- Turn the room lights on and have the remaining four students complete the demonstration, using the bulletin board to attach props as explained on the cue cards.
- As each student finishes an explanation, mount his or her cue card on the appropriate place on the display and link each picture to the next with string to show the position of our Solar System.
- Have students complete the data sheet How Fast Are You Traveling? When they have finished, discuss their answers and the motions of our planet.

Earth's Journey Cue Cards

1. **Earth rotates on its axis.**
   Simulation: Hold the globe in the light and point out the location of the people fastened to the equator and the location of your school. Slowly spin the globe west to east, showing that when the people are in the light, it is day. When they move around to the dark side, it is night. Show that it is day on one side of Earth and night on the other.

   Explain that the person at the equator travels at 1043 miles per hour (1669 kph).

   Props: globe, light, two cardboard people

2. **Earth orbits the sun at 66,660 mph.**
   Simulation: Hold the globe so the axis is always pointing in the same direction. Walk slowly around the light in a counterclockwise direction. Slowly spin the globe west to east to show day and night.

   Explain that the Earth travels around the sun once a year at 66,660 mph (106,656 kph).

   This takes 365 1/4 days, which we call a *year.*

   Props: globe, light

3. **Solar system is pulled toward Vega in the outer edge of the Milky Way Galaxy.**
   Simulation: Pin the solar system to the bulletin board. Show where Earth is located. Pin the Milky Way Galaxy to the bulletin board beside the solar system. Show that the sun is located near the outer edge of the Milky Way Galaxy. This is where our solar system is located as it is pulled toward the star Vega in this area.

   Explain that the speed of this motion toward Vega is 43,200 mph (69,120 kph).

   Props: solar system, Milky Way Galaxy

4. **The spiral shaped Milky Way Galaxy is rotating around a central cluster of stars.**
   Simulation: Spin the Milky Way Galaxy counterclockwise.

   Explain that the galaxy is spinning at 489,600 mph (783,360 kph).

   Our solar system moves with the spiral arms of the galaxy.

   Prop: Milky Way Galaxy

5. **The Milky Way Galaxy is pulled toward the Andromeda Galaxy in the Local Group.**
   Simulation: Pin the Local Group of Galaxies to the bulletin board and show the Andromeda Galaxy and the Milky Way Galaxy.

   Explain that the Milky Way Galaxy is being pulled at a speed of 180,000 mph (288,000 kph) toward the Andromeda Galaxy.

   Props: Milky Way Galaxy, Local Group

6. **The Local Group is pulled toward the Virgo Cluster in the Local Supercluster.**
   Simulation: Pin up the Local Supercluster of galaxies and show the location of the Local Group in it.

   Explain that the Local Group is being pulled at a speed of 540,000 mph (864,000 kph). Pin the Known Universe to the bulletin board and show the Local Supercluster. Everything in space is part of the Known Universe. Scientists are not sure if the Universe is in motion, but they feel certain that it is expanding.

   Props: Local Supercluster, Universe

Earth's Journey Models

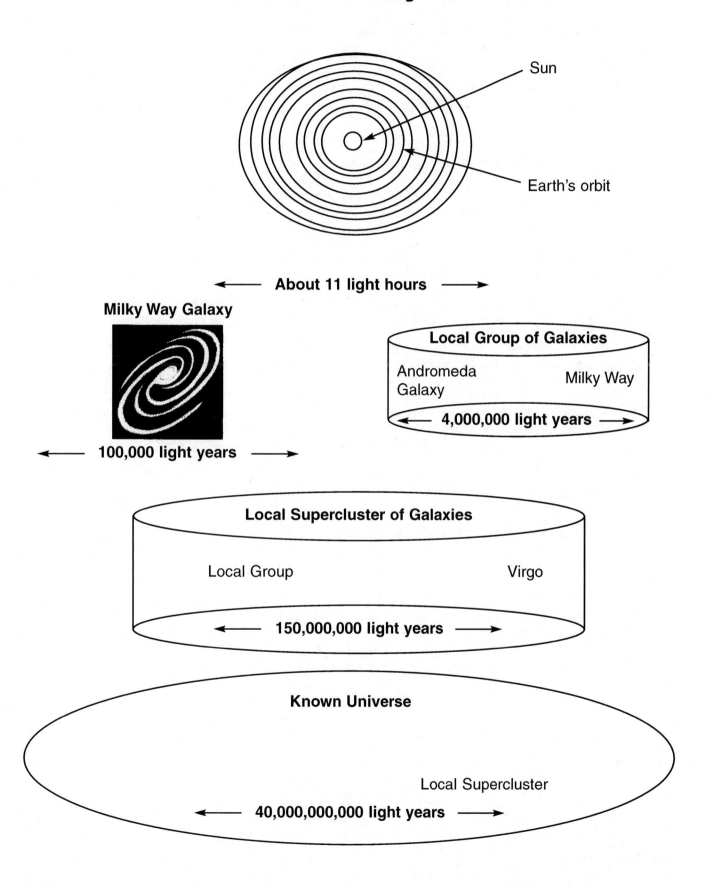

Sun

Earth's orbit

← About 11 light hours →

Milky Way Galaxy

100,000 light years →

Local Group of Galaxies

Andromeda Galaxy

Milky Way

← 4,000,000 light years →

Local Supercluster of Galaxies

Local Group

Virgo

← 150,000,000 light years →

Known Universe

Local Supercluster

← 40,000,000,000 light years →

How Fast Are You Traveling?

As we sit on this third planet from the sun, which we call Earth, we feel no motion. For that reason, long ago when people watched the sun, moon, and stars move in the sky, it looked as if they were all traveling east to west around Earth. Today, we know that only the moon travels around Earth; the daily motion of the sun and stars is caused by Earth's rotation on its axis once every 24 hours. The gradual change of the sun's position, as well as that of the constellations, is due to Earth's 365-day trip around the sun.

Summary of Earth's Speed Through the Universe

1. Earth rotates once on its axis every 24 hours. Earth's circumference at the equator is 25,035 miles (40,056 km). If we divide the distance by 24 hours, we discover that a person standing at the equator would be traveling at about 1,043 miles per hour (1,669 kph).

2. As Earth is spinning, it also moves around the sun. This trip takes about 365 days, moving at a speed of 66,660 mph (106,656 kph).

3. Our solar system consists of Earth and eight other planets in orbit around the sun. The solar system is traveling toward the star Vega at 43,200 mph (69,120 kph).

4. The solar system and Vega are located in the spiral Milky Way Galaxy near the outer edge. This galaxy looks like a pinwheel rotating at 489,600 mph (783,360 kph).

5. It was discovered in the 1920s that our Milky Way Galaxy was not the only one in the universe. The Milky Way Galaxy is moving toward the great Andromeda Galaxy at 180,000 mph (288,000 kph). The oval-shaped Andromeda Galaxy is part of the Local Group of galaxies.

6. The Local Group of Galaxies is being pulled toward the constellation Virgo. Virgo is located in the Local Supercluster of Galaxies. The Local Group is moving at a rate of 540,000 mph (864,000 kph).

Calculate Earth's Total Speed Through the Universe

1. Earth rotates around its axis at   <u>   1,043 mph   </u>

2. Earth revolves around the sun at   <u>   </u>

3. Our solar system travels toward Vega at   <u>   </u>

4. The solar system moves around the Milky Way Galaxy at   <u>   </u>

5. The Milky Way Galaxy falls toward Andromeda at   <u>   </u>

6. The Local Group is pulled toward the Local Supercluster at   <u>   </u>

Earth is traveling at   <u>   </u>

Finally, the universe is made up of the Local Group, as well as other galaxies and quasars. Scientists are not sure if the Universe is rotating. If it is, there would be more speed added. So, as you sit there as still as possible, are you really motionless?

Appendix

Planetary Facts

Categories	Mercury	Venus	Earth	Mars	Jupiter	Saturn	Uranus	Neptune	Pluto
Diameter in miles: (kilometers)	3,032 (4,879)	7,521 (12,104)	7,926 (12,756)	4,222 (6,794)	88,846 (142,984)	74,897 (120,536)	31,763 (51,118)	30,775 49,528	1,485 (2,390)
Diameters relative to Earth's:	.38	.95	1.0	.53	11.2	9.4	4	3.9	.18
Average distance from sun in millions of miles: (kilometers)	36 (58)	67 (108)	93 (150)	142 (228)	484 (779)	891 (1,434)	1,785 (2,873)	2,793 (4,495)	3,647 (5,870)
Relative to Earth's distance from the sun:	0.4 AU*	0.7 AU*	1.0 AU*	1.5 AU*	5.2 AU*	9.6 AU*	19.2 AU*	30 AU*	39.3 AU*
Length of year (trip around the sun):	88 days	224.7 days	365.3 days	687 days	11.86 years	29.46 years	84 years	165 years	248 years
Length of day (turn around once on axis):	59 days	243 days Retro**	23 h. 56 min.	24 h. 37 min.	9 h. 55 min.	10 h. 40 min.	17 h. 18 min. Retro**	16 h. 7 min.	6 days 9 h. 18 min. Retro**
Gravity at surface:	.38 g	.91 g	1.0 g	.38 g	2.36 g	.92 g	.89	1.12 g	.06 g
Number of moons:	0	0	1	2	28	30	21	8	1
Number of rings:	0	0	0	0	3	1,000 (?)	11	4	0

*AU = Astronomical Unit, average distance between Earth and sun is 93 million miles (149.6 million kilometers). The data below each planet shows its distance in astronomical units.

**Retro = retrograde or backwards motion from the rest of the planets. Earth turns (rotates) on its axis from west to east; planets which have retrograde motion rotate east to west.

These statistics were taken from the most recent information available from NASA and other reliable sources. You may find different data in more recent articles since this information is continuously being revised through the use of new equipment.

Resources

Related Books and Periodicals

Cole, Joanna. *The Magic School Bus® Lost in the Solar System.* Scholastic, Inc., 1990. This delightful book takes children on a unique field trip through the solar system aboard the Magic School Bus. They travel past each of the nine planets and the asteroid belt.

Dickinson, Terence. *Exploring the Night Sky.* Firefly Books, 1987. This is an award-winning children's book which takes a step-by-step cosmic voyage from Earth to a distance of 300 million light years, as well as providing detailed investigations of the planets and information about observing constellations.

Gallant, Roy A. *Our Universe.* National Geographic, 1994. (800) 447-0647. This outstanding picture atlas includes chapters for each of the planets, illustrated with NASA photographs and excellent information, as well as deep space objects, shuttles, and future space exploration.

Mammana, Dennis. *The Night Sky.* Running Press, 1989. This book provides interesting and easy-to-do investigations and observations of the constellations, planets, moon, and stars.

Newcott, W. B. "The Age of Comets." *National Geographic*, December, 1997. Here is an outstanding article describing Comet Hale-Bopp and many other famous comets. It includes information about the Shoemaker-Levy 9 comet which struck Jupiter. Also, it has a graphic showing Hale-Bopp's orbit and photo of the comet's nucleus taken by the satellite Giotto.

Sutton, Debra, et. al. *Moons of Jupiter*, 1993. Great Explorations in Math and Science [GEMS], Lawrence Hall of Science. Order from NSTA; see Materials sections. This contains activities for grades 4-9 to investigate and study Jupiter's moons.

VanCleave, Janice. *Astronomy for Every Kid.* John Wiley & Sons, Inc., 1991. Included are activities and projects with a list of materials, instructions, expected results, and explanations.

Young, Greg. *Exploring Mars* (Challenging). Teacher Created Resources, Inc., 1997. (800) 662-4321. This teacher's guide includes hands-on activities related to the *Mars Pathfinder* and *Mars Global Surveyor* missions for students in grades 5-7.

Young, Ruth M. *Science/Literature Unit: The Magic School Bus® Lost in the Solar System.* Teacher Created Resources, Inc., 1996. (800) 662-4321. This teachers' guide contains a variety of hands-on activities to teach astronomy concepts, including a script for a simulation flight to a station on the moon.

Young, Ruth M. *Science Simulations* (Challenging). Teacher Created Resources, Inc., 1997. (800) 662-4321. Simulations include a trip to Mars in the year 2025, as well as communicating with intelligent life beyond our solar system.

Young, Ruth M. *Space* (Intermediate). Teacher Created Resources, Inc., 1994. (800) 662-4321. This book contains activities related to the solar system, moon, tides, and space travel.

Resources *(cont.)*

Related Materials

Astronomical Society of the Pacific, 390 Ashton Ave., San Francisco, CA 94112. (800) 335-2624.

> http: //www.aspsky.org/html/tnl/tnl.html

They publish the quarterly newsletter *The Universe in the Classroom*, which has a different topic each issue with background information and lesson ideas. Free to teachers. Also supplies materials such as Mars map, booklets, posters, and slides of planets. Request free catalog.

Aurora Color Television Project, Geophysical Institute's GeoData Center (907) 474-7487. The Aurora Color Television Project uses a uniquely sensitive video camera capable of accurately representing the vivid, shifting colors and dynamic motion of spectacular auroral displays. Examples of the videotapes of aurora which are for purchase may be seen at the following site:

> http://www.pfrr.alaska.edu/actp/INDEX.HTM

Delta Education, P.O. Box 3000, Nashua, NH 03071-3000. (800) 442-5444. Supplies science materials, including magnets, solar system mobile, videos, and an astronomical hands-on kit.

Jet Propulsion Laboratory (JPL), Mail Stop CS-530, 4800 Oak Grove Drive, Pasadena, CA 90090. (818) 354-6111. Here is a source of videotapes and pictures on a wide range of topics related to Mars exploration. The video JPL *Computer Graphics* (100 minutes) includes an animation of a flight over Mars, taken from the data gathered during the Viking missions. Excellent photographs are available with information on the Mars missions. Contact the Teacher Resource Center at JPL and request that they send material they have on the Mars explorations.

NASA's Central Operation of Resources for Educators (CORE), Lorain County JVS, 15181 Route 28 South, Oberlin, OH 44074. (216) 774-1051, Ext. 293. Online catalog at:

> http://core.nasa.gov/

Provides material from NASA to use with students, including: slides, videos, and photographs taken from satellites and space missions. Write on school letterhead to request a free catalog and information regarding certification to borrow moon rock specimens.

National Geographic Society, P.O. Box 2118, Washington, D.C. 20013-2118. (800) 447-0647. Web site homepage:

> http://www.nationalgeographic.com/

Supplies maps and posters such as The Heavens, The Earth's Moon, Solar System/Celestial Family, and The Universe. Back issues of National Geographic may be ordered by telephone.

National Science Teachers Association (NSTA). (800) 722 NSTA. Supplies, books, posters, and CDROM related to astronomy and other sciences. Order a free catalog.

The Planetary Society, 65 North Catalina Ave., Pasadena, CA 91106-9899. (818) 793-5100. Order the 25 x 24 inch map of Mars—*An Explorer's Guide to Mars*. This map shows details of the planet, as well as pictures from Viking 1 and 2 missions. Request a catalog of other materials.

Sky Calendar, illustrated monthly calendar of daily astronomical events. Annual subscription is available from Abrams Planetarium, Michigan State University, East Lansing, MI 48824.

Answer Key

Plotting Planetary Orbital Distances (page 7)

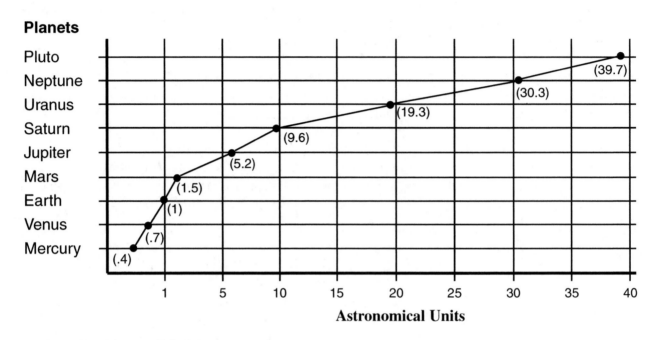

How Fast Do Planets Spin? (page 13)

Circumference	÷	Diameter	=	Results
Circle 1 = 15.5 cm		5 cm		3.10
Circle 2 = 25.3 cm		8 cm		3.16
Circle 3 = 38 cm		12 cm		3.16

Note: The results will vary. When the results are averaged, they should equal about 3.14. Diameter of Earth 7,973 miles x 3.14 = 25,035 miles (circumference) ÷ 24 hours = 1,043 mph.

Rotation Speed of Planets

	Mercury	Venus	Earth	Mars	Jupiter	Saturn	Uranus	Neptune	Pluto
Diameter in Miles: kilometers)	3,050 (4,880)	7,565 (12,104)	7,973 (12,756)	4,246 (6,794)	89,365 (142,984)	75,335 (120,536)	31,948 (51,117)	30,933 (49,493	1,421 (2,274)
Circumference in Miles (kilometers)	9,577 (15,323)	23,754 (38,006)	25,035 (40,056)	13,332 (21,333)	280,606 (448,970)	236,552 (378,483)	100,317 (160,507)	97,130 (155,408)	4,462 (7,139)
Length of Day in Hours	1416 h	5,832 h	24 h	25 h	10h	I I h	17 h	16 h	153 h
Rotation Speed mph (kph)	7 (11)	4 (6)	1,043 (1669)	533 (853)	28,061 (44,898)	21,505 (34,408)	5,901 (9,442)	6, 071 (9,714)	29 (46)

Answer Key *(cont.)*

The Moon on the Net (pages 26 and 27)

Moon Introduction (page 26)

1. bright highlands and darker plains
2. craters
3. less dense
4. Neil Armstrong, July 20, 1969
5. by radio
6. No, there would be no sound since there is no atmosphere on the moon to carry the sound.
7. The sky would be black since there is no atmosphere surrounding the moon. The blue sky on Earth is caused by molecules of atmospheric gases scattering sunlight. Gravity is 1/6th that of Earth's, so it would be much easier to move around.
8. The moon rotates on its axis the same length of time it takes it to revolve once around Earth—27 days, 7 hours, and 43 minutes.
9. Seismic stations were left on the moon and could detect moonquakes. As with earthquakes, geologists can use the rate of speed with which moonquakes travel to determine what the interior is like.
10. Yes, these are caused by meteor impacts, or impacts from deliberately crashing the *Lunar Module* into the moon.
11. The moon's crust is nearly 10% thicker than Earth's.
12. No, it is not an iron-rich core like Earth's.
13. It is at least 4.6 billion years. We know this from the rock samples brought back by the *Apollo* astronauts.
14. No, it is considered geologically dead.

Views of the Moon (page 27)

1. The moon is divided into the crust, mantle, and core. The lunar crust thickness varies from tens of kilometers in depth under the mare to more than 100 kilometers in some highland regions, with an average thickness of about 70 kilometers. The core radius is between 300 and 425 kilometers.
2. They saw the full moon and got a good view of the light (highlands) and dark (mare) areas.
3. Red areas are usually lunar highlands; blue to orange are the ancient volcanic lava flow of a mare, or lunar sea. Bluer mare areas contain more titanium than do the orange regions. Blue and orange areas covering much of the left side of the Moon are separate lava flows in Oceanus Procellarum. Small purple areas found near the center are deposits formed by explosive volcanic eruptions. The fresh crater Tycho is prominent at the bottom of the photograph.
4. They saw that it is heavily cratered. The far side of the moon faces the oncoming meteors; some meteors which were on the way to the moon may have been pulled into Earth. Thus, more craters were formed on the far side.
5. They show a major depression near the lunar south pole (center), which is probably an ancient basin formed by the impact of an asteroid or comet. A significant portion of the dark area near the pole may be in permanent shadow and sufficiently cold to trap water from a comet in the form of ice. The impact basin Schrodinger is a two-ring basin that is recognized to be the second youngest impact basin on the moon. Its center is flooded by lava. A volcanic vent seen in the floor of the crater is one of the largest single explosive volcanoes on the moon.
6. waning gibbous; yes
7. It has seats for two, large tires, no cover, dish antenna, and fenders over the wheels. There are footprints in the soil from the astronauts. The lunar soil is very fine, so the fenders are to keep the dust from flying up onto the passengers and equipment.
8. black; waning quarter; waxing quarter
9. The orange glass spheres and fragments are the finest particles, ranging in size from 20 to 45 microns, about the same size as silt on Earth. Chemical analysis of the orange soil showed it to be similar to some of the samples brought back from *Apollo 11*. It is rich in titanium (8%) and iron oxide (22%). But unlike the *Apollo 11* samples, the orange soil is unexplainably rich in zinc. The orange soil is probably of volcanic origin and not the product of meteorite impact.

Answer Key *(cont.)*

Comparing Sunspots to Magnetic Disturbances—1897 to 1980 (page 41)

When there were fewer sunspots, there were also fewer magnetic disturbances. The sunspot activity cycle is 11 years, just like the magnetic disturbances. This is clear evidence that there is a correlation between the amount of solar activity and magnetic disturbances on Earth.

Cycle of the Sunspots (page 42)

Years of Least Magnetic Disturbances

Years	Period between Years
1879	
1891	12
1902	11
1914	12
1925	11
1935	10
1946	11
1955	9
1966	11
1978	12
	Total 99

99	**÷ 9**	**= 11**
Total Years	Total Periods	Average Period

1. Summary: There is an 11-year cycle of years with the least magnetic disturbances.

2. The overall level of magnetic disturbance from year to year has increased substantially from a low around 1900. Also, the average of each year's highs and lows is now much higher, so that a year which should have minimum magnetic disturbances now is typically more disturbed than years at maximum disturbance levels before 1900.

Comet Halley (page 48)

1. 76 years
2. 2061
3. 239 B.C., 11 B.C., 66 A.D., 451, and 1066 A.D.
4. Halley's orbit is retrograde (backwards) to the orbits of the planets around the sun. It is inclined 18° to the ecliptic, more than even Pluto.
5. Five spacecraft from USSR, Japan, and Europe visited it; Giotto took photos of it.
6. The nucleus is 16 x 8 x 8 km and darker than coal. It is not very dense; mostly dust remains. Other answers will vary.

How Fast Are You Traveling? (page 74)
Earth's total speed through the Universe is 1,320,503 mph (2,128,805 kph).